Hour of Power
Moving Your Prayer Life to the Next Level

Mary A. Ford

All scripture quotations, unless otherwise indicated, are from the following Bible versions:

New King James Version (NKJV)
Scripture taken from the New King James Version®. Copyright © 1982 by Thomas Nelson. Used by permission. All rights reserved.

American Standard Version (ASV)
Used under standard copyright law of Public Domain. Last copyright 1901.

Easy-to-Read Version (ERV)
Copyright © 2006 by World Bible Translation Center.

New International Version (NIV)
THE HOLY BIBLE, NEW INTERNATIONAL VERSION®, NIV® Copyright © 1973, 1978, 1984, 2011 by Biblica, Inc. ® Used by permission. All rights reserved worldwide.

Also acknowledging the influence of many spiritual writers along the way on the subject of prayer. I am particularly grateful to Dick Eastman, author of *The Hour That Changes the World,* publisher Chosen Books, 2002.

Any omission of credits is unintentional.
Content in this book may not necessarily represent the thoughts and beliefs of Radical Women.

©Copyright 2017 by Mary A. Ford – Duty2Delight Ministries.
www.duty2delightministries.com
All Rights Reserved

Publisher: bylisabell
Radical Women (DBA)
PO Box 782
Granbury, TX 76048
www.bylisabell.com

ISBN 10: 0998330833
ISBN 13: 978-0998330839

DEDICATION

This book, *Hour of Power: Moving Your Prayer Life to the Next Level* is dedicated in loving memory of my beloved parents, Leon and Furlisha Coronado; my eldest sister, Barbara J. Simpson; and my mother-in-love, Dean Ford. Although they are absent from their mortal bodies and present with the Lord, the legacy of their love, prayers and family devotion lives on.

This book is also dedicated to all the "seasoned saints" who left the prints of their praying hands on my life as a young child. The imagery of their passionate, persistent and powerful prayers still lingers on today in my memory—and in my soul.

~Rest in Heaven Until We Meet Again~

Table of Contents

INTRODUCTION i
GOALS & OBJECTIVES iii
The Challenge iv
PRE-PRAYER QUIZ v
Five Basic Lessons on Prayer 1
   Lesson 1: What Is Prayer? 2
      Time With God Prayer Agenda 8
      A Personal Prayer of Repentance 9
   Lesson 2: What Prayer Does 10
      Time With God Prayer Agenda 12
      A Personal Prayer of Surrender 13
   Lesson 3: What's Hindering Your Prayers? 14
      Time With God Prayer Agenda 16
      A Personal Prayer of Faith 17
   Lesson 4: What Effective Prayer Requires 18
      Time With God Prayer Agenda 19
      A Personal Prayer of Commitment 20
   Lesson 5: How Do We Get Started? 21
      Time With God Prayer Agenda 24
      A Personal Prayer of Consistency 25
A Twelve Step Personal Prayer Plan 26
   INDEX 26
   A Twelve Step Personal Prayer Plan 27
   Step 1 ~ Adoration 28
      Time With God Prayer Agenda 34
      A Personal Prayer of Adoration 35
   Step 2 ~ Confession 36

Time With God Prayer Agenda	38
A Personal Prayer to Admit Your Guilt	39
Step 3 ~ Thanksgiving	40
Morning Prayer of Thanksgiving	43
Time With God Prayer Agenda	44
Step 4 ~ Supplication	45
Time With God Prayer Agenda	47
A Personal Prayer of Petition	48
Step 5 ~ Waiting	49
Time With God Prayer Agenda	51
A Personal Prayer of Surrender	52
Step 6 ~ Watching	53
Time With God Prayer Agenda	56
A Personal Prayer for Holy Alertness	57
Step 7 ~ Intercession	58
Take the 4 x 4 Challenge!	61
Time With God Prayer Agenda	62
A Personal Prayer of Intercession	63
Step 8 ~ Praying the Scriptures	64
Time With God Prayer Agenda	67
A Personal Prayer Pleading God's Promises	69
Step 9 ~ Serenading God	70
Time With God Prayer Agenda	72
A Personal Song of Prayer	73
Step 10 ~ Meditation	74
Time With God Prayer Agenda	78
A Prayer of Meditation	79
Step 11 ~ Listening	80
Time With God Prayer Agenda	83
A Prayer Time of Listening	84
Step 12 ~ Total Praise!	85

Time With God Prayer Agenda 86
A Personal Prayer of Praise & Worship 87
POST-PRAYER QUIZ 88
Five Lessons on Prayer Answer Keys 90
Twelve Step Personal Prayer Plan Answer Keys 96
About The Author 110
Testimonials ~ What They Say About Mary 113

INTRODUCTION

    Do you agree that in order to have a good marriage, a thriving business, or a fulfilling relationship—*it takes work?* What about raising a family, managing a household, or establishing a successful career—do these things take work? Think about what "kind" of work it takes to accomplish or experience success in these areas of life that we deem as being important. Think about things like patience, sacrifice, submission, self-control, tenacity, courage, perseverance and faith—just to name a few. These things do not come easily for most of us. As a result, we must step outside of our comfort zone and put forth great effort to accomplish them.

    After considering what it takes to be successful in these various avenues of life, what do you think it takes to have a powerful, fervent and effective prayer life? Yes, you got it—WORK! Just like successful marriages, relationships, businesses and careers take work—having a powerful, fervent and effective prayer life takes work. The Apostle Paul said it like this*: "I entreat you, brethren, for the sake of our Lord Jesus Christ and by the love given by the Spirit, to unite with me in earnest wrestling in prayer to God in my behalf."* (Romans 15:30)

    Scripture tells us that it takes effort (work) to have an effective, powerful and fervent prayer life—but this work is a labor of love. This labor of love not only allows us to intercede and petition God on behalf of ourselves and others, it also enables the believer to grow in intimacy with the Father and serves as the vehicle Christians use to enter into the very presence of God! *"Confess your sins to one another, and pray for one another, that you may be healed. The effectual fervent prayer of a righteous man avails much."* (James 5:16)

    This book, *Hour of Power: Moving Your Prayer Life to the Next Level*, will encourage Christians to cultivate a more powerful, purposeful and effective prayer life through spending dedicated, consistent, intimate time with the lover of their souls—*and truly enjoy it!* Through applying practical prayer principles and exercising the range of prayer components found in this book, your prayer life will grow stronger and your time spent with God sweeter as you experience a deeper and more intimate relationship with God through the power of *PRAYER!*

Enjoy Your Journey!
Mary A. Ford

*"The effective, fervent prayer
of a righteous man avails much."*
(James 5:16)

GOALS & OBJECTIVES

GOALS

The overall goal of this book is to strengthen the spiritual resolve of the believer and encourage a transformed walk with Christ through the enrichment of personal prayer. This scripture based prayer curriculum is designed to:

- ❖ Spiritually equip Christians to pray more powerfully and effectively.
- ❖ Nurture a more intimate relationship with God through spending quality time with Him in the study and application of his word and prayer.

OBJECTIVES

Applying the lessons and prayer principles contained in this study guide will result in a more powerful, passionate, purposeful and effective prayer life while growing deeper in intimacy with God. Christians will:

- ❖ Be challenged to make prayer a daily priority through integrating a variety of prayer principles and techniques into personal prayer time.
- ❖ Develop consistency in their prayer life through establishing a specific time and place for prayer—daily.
- ❖ Be encouraged to increase personal prayer time with God by learning how to pray all types of prayers.
- ❖ Cultivate a desire to pray—longing to be in the presence of the Father more and more each day.

The Challenge

Most Christians pray—at least at some time or another! For many believers, their prayer lives consist of a few scattered prayers here and there—most spurred on by some current circumstance, situation or predicament. But how many believers have actually reached the spiritual plateau of spending at least an hour in prayer daily—*and enjoy it?*

Well, you might ask, "What's the big deal about spending an hour in prayer?" Or, you may be thinking, "Why set an hour as my daily goal?" The best answer to these questions is this—Jesus is the perfect role model (example) for living the Christian life. He spent much time in personal prayer, and spoke of the one-hour timeframe in Matthew 26:40-41 where he pleaded with his disciples. *"Could you not watch with me for just one hour? Watch and pray, lest you enter into temptation. The spirit indeed is willing, but the flesh is weak."*

Yes, even Jesus spent dedicated time in daily prayer. He knew the value of praying—being in consistent, intimate contact and communion with his Father—not only to remain in God's will, but also in order to fight off the attacks of the enemy from without and within.

As those who wear the name of Christ, we must "model Christ" in every way—even in prayer. Although many Christians settle their scope of praying around the four basic "types" of prayer—adoration, confession, thanksgiving, and petition—this study guide, *Hour of Power: Moving Your Prayer Life to the Next Level,* challenges the believer to expand personal prayer practices well beyond these four basic elements. In fact, this study guide will escort you into a realm of prayer where you will experience a deeper, richer and more intimate daily prayer and devotional time—causing your personal prayer life to catapult into the next level of intimacy with God!

As you begin this journey, and endeavor to accomplish your personal spiritual goals and objectives, be assured that the Holy Spirit awaits to help unlock the treasures you seek as you spend more, intimate time with God through His Word and personal daily prayer. As you study, pray and apply the lessons you learn along the way, you will find your personal prayer time growing stronger and sweeter day-by-day. You begin to truly enjoy Jesus!

Therefore, I encourage and challenge you to open up the channels of your mind and allow God to speak to your heart in ways never experienced before. Expect a supernatural change in your prayer life—and in your overall desire for more of Jesus in your daily living. Welcome the Holy Spirit to do his perfect work *in* you, *to* you, and *through* you! Don't wait another minute—starting right now, pray for God to loosen the shackles of your mind and set you free from the ordinary. Pray for the Father to open up your heart, eyes and ears—then listen to what the Spirit has to say as you journey through the next eight weeks of prayer.

I ACCEPT THE CHALLENGE

_____   _____
(Signature)   (Date)

PRE-PRAYER QUIZ

INSTRUCTIONS: Think about your personal prayer life and where you are right now in it. Then take this short prayer quiz. Please be *totally honest* with your answers.

1. I would rate myself as a _____ on a scale of 1 to 10 as a prayer intercessor or a person of prayer. (1 is lowest and 10 is highest)

2. My spouse (or best friend) would give me a _____ on a scale of 1 to 10 as a prayer intercessor or a person of prayer based on what they know, and what I share about my prayer life. (1 is lowest and 10 is highest)

3. If I were to add up all the time I spent praying today (alone or in a group) my total time would be _____ (approximately).

4. My main reason for praying is: (only circle <u>one</u> answer)

    a) To get something from God.
    b) To just enjoy time with God.
    c) To pray for someone I love.
    d) To check it off on my daily "To Do List."

5. I find myself praying more often *when...* (complete this sentence)
   _____
   _____

6. I probably *don't* pray more because: (circle <u>ALL</u> that apply)
    a) I'm just too busy; not enough time.
    b) I'm too tired to really focus.
    c) It's boring to me.
    d) I don't really know how to pray.
    e) No one else in my house prays.
    f) I don't believe it makes a difference *or* that prayer works.
    g) _____
       (You fill in the blank above)

Five Basic Lessons on Prayer

"If my people, who are called by my name, will humble themselves and pray, And seek my face, and turn from their wicked ways, then I will hear from heaven, and I will forgive their sin and will heal their land"
(2 Chronicles 7:14)

Moving Your Prayer Life to the Next Level

Lesson 1: What Is Prayer?

When most think about prayer, the mind quickly resolves to petitioning a higher, more powerful, authoritative being in order to meet specific needs, desires or wants as life situations and circumstances are encountered. But shouldn't there be more to this thing we call prayer?

For the Christian, such things as patience, perseverance, persistence, fervency and faith are most important in developing an effective prayer life. Prayer is both simple and complex—both profound and humble. *But the soul of prayer begins with—the heart.*

I. **Let's start with the basics. First, define what you believe prayer *is* and what you believe prayer is *not*:**

   A. Prayer *IS*:

   _____
   _____
   _____
   _____
   _____

   B. Prayer is *NOT*:

   _____
   _____
   _____
   _____
   _____

II. **Pleading vs. Begging**

Many believers mistake "begging" for "pleading" when it comes to prayer. Though they are similar in meaning, there is a methodical difference between the two when considering the realm of prayer. Begging, on one hand, usually consists of repetitious soliciting—usually asking for something for which there is a strong desire to acquire, but presents no evidence to support the request—its intent is to simply wear down the listener in hopes to receive whatever is desired. On the other hand, pleading is a heartfelt petition or appeal for something or someone in an urgent and/or emotional way—its intent is to state ones case while presenting facts or evidence in hopes to sway the listener in their favor.

For instance, a lawyer in a courtroom doesn't "beg" your case by saying over and over... "Oh please, please, please judge. Don't convict my client!" No—that would be useless. Rather, an effective lawyer "pleads" your case before the judge or jury. Based on facts, motive, evidence and clearly established just cause—the odds of things going in your favor will be much greater. That type of an appeal will surely get the judge or jury's attention—possibly resulting in a positive outcome for the defendant. Likewise, prayer allows us to plead our concerns to God through His son Jesus. No matter what the situation looks like or what the circumstance may predict—prayer allows us to appeal to a higher court!

A. Prayer is *c*_____, *c*_____, *c*_____, and *fellowship* with the living God.

B. Effective prayer involves *t*_____ and *l*_____. Prayer is a two-way dialogue—not just *m*_____!

C. No matter how bleak your situation or circumstance may be—you can always go to God in prayer knowing that Jesus is your *r*_____ judge who will hear your every *p*_____!

"Thus says the Lord who made it, the Lord who formed it to establish it (the Lord is His name): 'Call to Me, and I will answer you, and show you great and mighty things, which you do not know'" (Jeremiah 33:2-3).

❧ Notes ❧

III. The Importance of Humility

Having a humble spirit is a prerequisite to powerful, effective prayer. In 2 Chronicles 7:14, God lists "humility" as the first condition to Him hearing and answering our prayers… *"If my people, who are called by my name, will **humble themselves and pray…**"*

  A. Humility is the result of having a *h*_____ surrendered to God. Trusting and depending totally upon God to work things out instead of relying on personal resources, worldly connections, and tangible possessions.

  B. On the other hand, when your focus is taken off *G*_____ and put on yourself—overemphasizing self rather than God—that's pride.

  C. Humility and *p*_____ cannot occupy the same space within your heart—nor can powerful, effective prayers come from prideful lips.

  D. A heart completely *s*_____ to God does not attempt to use prayer to manipulate people and force personal agendas in order to control situations and circumstances. A surrendered heart humbly s_____ your will to God's sovereign plans in prayer. *"Father, if it is your will, take this cup away from me; nevertheless not my will, but yours, be done"* (Luke 22:42).

❧ Notes ❧

_____
_____
_____
_____
_____
_____
_____
_____
_____
_____

IV. Seeking God's Face vs. His Hand

Effective prayer is not begging, bargaining, or giving ultimatums to God. Nor should prayer minimize God to a *"big vending machine in the sky"* where Christians can *"put in a prayer and pull out a blessing."* No. Prayer was never intended to be reduced to simply a way for believers to get things *from God*—but rather prayer was designed as the way for believers to get *to God*.

Now, this certainly does not mean that we should never petition God for the desires of our hearts. In fact, the bible encourages us to ask for what we need and seek God's provision in prayer. (Matthew 7:7) But what father would be pleased with a child that only came to him when they wanted or needed something? God desires a *complete* and *intimate* <u>relationship</u> with each of His children.

    A. Relationship with God requires the believer to go much deeper in prayer than mere ***p*_____**. It requires intimacy—true ***c*_____** with the Father.

    B. Relationship with God goes beyond simply to know "about God," but rather it is predicated on getting to *"know God"* on a ***p*_____** level.

    C. Relationship with God means the believer's prayers must not always be focused on seeking God's ***h*_____** (presents), but rather intimate, effective prayer involves humbly seeking God's ***f*_____** (presence)—desperately desiring God's will, presence, and power in your daily life.

*"If My people who are called by My name, will **humble** themselves, and **pray,** and **seek My face…**"* (2 Chronicles 7: 14)

❧ Notes ❧

_____
_____
_____
_____
_____
_____
_____
_____
_____
_____
_____

V.   **The Power of Repentance**

God is not so much concerned about the words we use in prayer as He is the condition of our hearts. *"Therefore the Lord said: "In as much as these people draw near with their mouths and honor Me with their lips, But have removed their hearts far from Me"* (Isaiah 29:13). Heartfelt prayer transcends mere words—it allows us to climb up into the safety of our heavenly Father's arms, lay our weary heads upon His chest, and tell Him all about our troubles, trials and triumphs!

Prayer is a gracious gift of God that allows us to step out of time into eternity and enter into the very presence of our Most High God! Yes indeed, prayer is a *gift* from God to mankind. But prayer is much more than what many believers know. Prayer is a divine power, rooted and grounded in God's omnipotence! What a wonderful gift! But there are some *conditions* to the believer receiving the promise of God's presence and power in our lives when we pray.

A. Humility and seeking God's will in prayer are certainly at the top of the list—however, we must never neglect the necessity of *r_____* in prayer. In Psalms 51:1-12 King David prayed a powerful prayer of repentance after he had committed adultery with Bathsheba. The prophet Nathan made him brutally aware of the condition of his unrepentant heart and the consequences thereof.

> *"Have mercy on me, O God, according to your unfailing love; according to your great compassion blot out my transgressions. Wash away all my iniquity and cleanse me from my sin. For I know my transgressions, and my sin is always before me. Against you, you only, have I sinned and done what is evil in your sight; so you are right in your verdict and justified when you judge. Surely, I was sinful at birth, sinful from the time my mother conceived me.*
>
> *Yet you desired faithfulness even in the womb; you taught me wisdom in that secret place. Cleanse me with hyssop, and I will be clean; wash me, and I will be whiter than snow. Let me hear joy and gladness; let the bones you have crushed rejoice. Hide your face from my sins and blot out all my iniquity. Create in me a pure heart, O God, and renew a steadfast spirit within me. Do not cast me from your presence or take your Holy Spirit from me. Restore to me the joy of your salvation and grant me a willing spirit, to sustain me."*

B. *C_____* without *r_____* has no power. True repentance requires the believer to say *"I'm sorry, Lord"*—then turn *a_____* from sinful habits and turn *t_____* a forgiving Savior!

C. The power of *r_____* paves the path to heavens blessings! *"...and turn from their wicked ways, then I will hear from heaven, and will forgive their sin and heal their land"* (2 Chronicles 7:14).

❧ Notes ❧

Time With God Prayer Agenda

"When led by the Spirit, the child of God must be as ready to wait as to go, as prepared to be silent as to speak—and above all prepared to obey."

I. **Period of Confession**—*silently read Psalms 66:17-20.*

II. **Prayer Focuses**—*Pray for the following:*
   A. To know God in a more *intimate* way. (John 14:17)
   B. That you will not *grieve* the Holy Spirit. (Hebrews 10:29)
   C. The Holy Spirit will *reveal* to you any *sin* in your life (e.g. deceitfulness, hypocrisy, unbelief, ungratefulness, worry, bitterness, unforgiveness, pride, etc.)—then earnestly *confess* and *repent*. (Romans 8:2)
   D. The Holy Spirit will help you to *release* your *faith* through believing prayer—trusting God at *all* times and in *all* circumstances. (2 Timothy 1:7)
   E. That God will teach you to *know his voice* and believe that He will guide you through the decisions and details of your life. (2 Corinthians 3:5)
   F. That God will *reveal* to you *His will* as you commit to a lifestyle of *prayer* and *study* of His word. (I Peter 4:14)

❧ *Spirit Inspired Thoughts* ❧

~A Personal Prayer of Repentance~

"In prayer, God hears more than just words…He listens to your heart. The power of Repentance paves the path to heavens blessings!"

Journal *your personal prayer of repentance* here. God is seeking a humble, *repentant* heart. Ask Him to forgive you of any known sin and give you strength to walk in His will—daily. Pray that God clearly reveals to you any way you may have unappreciated or misused the *gift* of prayer in the past. Thank God for making available such a wonderful *gift!* Ask God to draw you closer to Him as you spend more and more time in daily prayer.

Psalms 66:18

_____
_____
_____
_____
_____
_____
_____
_____
_____
_____
_____
_____
_____
_____
_____
_____
_____
_____

In Jesus' name I pray, Amen.

Lesson 2: What Prayer Does

Prayer is a wonderful gift of God—divinely designed for mankind! The apostle James tells us *"the effective, fervent prayer of a righteous man avails much."* (James 5:16b) But guess what? Satan wants to keep the believer from praying. Matter of fact, when Satan sees the weakest of saints on his or her knees in prayer—he begins to tremble. Why is this?

I. **What does prayer do that causes Satan to tremble and be afraid?**

   A. Prayer _____ us to the main _____ _____. (Jeremiah 33:3)

   B. Prayer gives us complete _____ to God's _____. (Philippians 4:13; Jeremiah 32:27; John 15:7)

   C. Prayer _____ us for spiritual _____. (Ephesians 6:11-12, 18)

      1. Prayer is a _____ _____ weapon!

      2. We cannot fight spiritual _____ with _____ weapons.

      3. We must learn how to _____ use our spiritual warfare weapons to fight-off the _____!

II. **Do you have your War Clothes on?**

   A. Are you *effectively* using your spiritual warfare weapons of *praise*, the _____, and _____ daily? (Ephesians 6:17-18)

   B. Developing an effective prayer life takes *patience, persistence, fervency* and *f*_____. (Philippians 4:13)

III. **Cast all your Cares—I Surrender All!**

   A. Prayer *lifts* our *b*_____ and frees us to praise God in advance! (1 Peter 5:7)

B. Prayer allows the believer to gain **_a_**_____ to God's divine power and fully equips us for spiritual **_w_**_____ as we practice total **_s_**_____. (Eph. 6:19)

C. Worry won't work, but **_p_**_____ will. You must *surrender* complete control of your life to God—then watch Him work it out! (Romans 8:28; James 5:16)

❧ Notes ❧

Time With God Prayer Agenda

"The only way to do battle with Satan is—on your knees!"

I. **Period of Confession**—silently confess before the Lord.

II. **Prayer Focuses—Pray for the following: (Romans 12:1-2)**
   A. Personal spiritual growth and Christian maturity.
   B. A desire to *care* about the things that God cares about.
   C. Spiritual *20/20*—see things, people and sin as God sees them.
   D. Learn to *choose* the things that God chooses.
   E. To become a passionate, persistent, fervent person of prayers that work!

❧ Spirit Inspired Thoughts ❧

~A Personal Prayer of Surrender~

"Don't agonize over the enemy's tactics—they can only forge the weapons, but God renders them ineffective. Worry Won't Work—Prayer Will!"

Journal *your personal prayer of surrender* here. You will know you're *surrendered* to God when you rely on Him to work things out instead of trying to manipulate others, force your own agenda, and control the situation. Ask God to show you areas in your life where you may need to grow, trust, release and relinquish any doubt, fear, anxiety or lack of faith. Pray and ask the Holy Spirit to help you let go and let God work!

Psalms 37:7

_____
_____
_____
_____
_____
_____
_____
_____
_____
_____
_____
_____
_____
_____
_____
_____

In Jesus' name I pray, Amen.

Lesson 3: What's Hindering Your Prayers?

So often believers feel their prayers are not going any higher than the ceiling. We pray and pray—but still no answers seem to come. We question if God really hears us when we pray—and then we begin to doubt if God truly cares about our current plight. We wonder—does He love us enough to deliver us from the pain, problem, or perpetual state of helplessness and hopelessness we seem to be falling deeper and deeper into?

The answer is a resounding YES! God invites us time and time again throughout scripture to *come* to Him (Matthew 11:28), *trust* Him (Proverbs 3:5), *try* Him (Malachi 3:10), and *call* to Him (Jeremiah 33:3) in prayer—*"Call to Me, and I will answer you, and show you great and mighty things, which you do not know."*

Scripture tells us God loves us and cares about every concern, situation, trial and tribulation that may come our way. *But,* He is most concerned about our *spiritual* condition, which often times can be the root cause of our current *physical* state.

These spiritual disorders can manifest themselves in our lives in various ways. And they can, and will, *hinder* the believers' prayers, rendering them ineffective.

I. **Let's look at some *hindrances* to praying effective prayers. After reading the reference scriptures below, write your thoughts concerning each hindrance:**
   A. Un-confessed *s*_____ (Micah 3:4)
   _____
   _____
   _____

   B. Lack of *f*_____ (James 1:6-7)
   _____
   _____
   _____

   C. Wrong *m*_____ (James 4:3)
   _____
   _____
   _____

D. Wrong *a*_____ (Luke 18:9-14)

_____
_____
_____
_____

II. **What's *hindering* your prayer life?** *Write your specific hindrances below:*
   A. _____
   B. _____
   C. _____
   D. _____
   E. _____

❧ *Notes* ❧

Time With God Prayer Agenda

"My only hope of Strength for this Journey is when My Heart and God's meet in Prayer"

I. Period of Confession—*silently read Psalm 103:12-14.*

II. Period of Petition—*Pray for the following personal petitions:*
   A. Personal spiritual growth and maturity.
   B. To *care* about the things that God *cares* about.
   C. To *see* things the way that God *sees* them.
   D. To *choose* the things that God *chooses*.
   E. To overcome any personal *hindrances* and become a *passionate*, *persistent*, *effective* person of prayer.

❧ Spirit Inspired Thoughts ❧

_____
_____
_____
_____
_____
_____
_____
_____
_____
_____

~A Personal Prayer of Faith~

"Don't tell God about your BIG problems—tell your problems about your BIG GOD!"

Journal *your personal prayer of faith* here. Pray for God to reveal any *hindrances* to your prayers—wrong motives, bad attitudes, sin nature, or lack of faith. Ask the Holy Spirit to help you *grow* past relying on what you *see* in the *natural* to believing what is *possible* in the *supernatural*. Pray for *BIG Faith!*

Hebrews 11:6

_____
_____
_____
_____
_____
_____
_____
_____
_____
_____
_____
_____
_____
_____
_____
_____
_____
_____

In Jesus' name I pray, Amen.

Lesson 4: What Effective Prayer Requires

In our previous lesson, we discovered our prayers can indeed be hindered, rendering them ineffective. Perhaps you have felt this way about your prayers on occasion—that they lacked power, zeal, fervency, and effectiveness. How does one have the kind of prayer life the apostle James spoke about?—*"The effective, fervent prayer of a righteous man avails much."* (James 5:16b) Cultivating an effective, fervent, powerful prayer life involves seeking, knocking, and searching for God's will—with all your heart!

Many times in prayer, we give up way too soon on God, becoming weary of waiting. But when a believer commits to seeking only God's will in prayer, it leads to abundant blessings! We must learn to practice P.U.S.H. (pray until something happens)—trusting and obeying God every step of the way. So, let's look at what it actually requires to cultivate a powerful, fervent and effective prayer life.

I. What does effective prayer require?
   A. Commitment—Effective prayer involves _____. It is a labor of _____.
      (Jeremiah 29:13; Genesis 32:24-26)
   B. Persistence—We must practice persistence in prayer by _____, _____, _____, and waiting until we get an answer and submit to God's will.
      (Luke 11:8-9; 18:2-8)
   C. Passion—Fervency is a condition of the _____. God wants us to care about the things He cares about—pray passionately!
      (James 5:16)
   D. Obedience—God wants us to be serious about seeking His _____ and not just His *presents*. He wants us to desire more of Him—not just His gifts!
      (Mark 13:33) (Luke 18:1) (I Thess. 5:17) (Col. 4:2)

II. **Prayer is NOT a s_____ *or* a c_____; but it's a c_____!**
    (Matthew 6:6). Journal your thoughts below concerning the meaning of this statement:
    _____
    _____
    _____

Time With God Prayer Agenda

"The Soul of Prayer Begins with—The Heart"

I. **Period of Confession**—cleansing your temple. (I John 1:9)

II. **Period of Meditation**—silently before the Lord. (Lamentations 3:22-26)

III. **Period of Praise and Thanksgiving:**
   A. Praise God for his love and for HIS readiness to have a "love relationship" with you.
   B. Thank God for giving you a desire to pray and for strengthening your prayer life.
   C. Praise God for HIS omnipotence, omniscience, and sovereignty.
   D. Thank God for HIS generosity in making the "gifts" of prayer available to you.

IV. Prayer Focuses—*Pray for the following:*
   A. Personal commitment and consistency in prayer—daily seeking God's presence, direction and guidance before getting involved in the day's activities.
   B. To exhibit passion, power and fervency when communing with God.
   C. To be obedient to God's commandment to pray—desiring more and more of Him!

❧ Spirit Inspired Thoughts ❧

_____
_____
_____
_____
_____
_____
_____
_____

~A Personal Prayer of Commitment~

"Prayer is NOT a Suggestion or a Choice—It's a Commandment"

Journal *your personal prayer of commitment* here. Ask the Holy Spirit to reveal areas in your life where you lack *commitment* and *obedience*. Practice *persistence* in praying for breakthroughs in areas that need to be strengthened. Pray for God to give you a zeal for His word and *fervency* in your prayers as you commit to seeking His face in every area of your life.

Psalm 37:5

_____
_____
_____
_____
_____
_____
_____
_____
_____
_____
_____
_____
_____
_____

In Jesus' name I pray, Amen.

Lesson 5: How Do We Get Started?

Most Christians pray. At least at some time or another. But perhaps you have developed some poor prayer habits along the way that have slowly strangled the life out of your personal prayer time. How does one excel past having a prayer life that consists of crisis prayers, boring repetition or praying only prayers of petition to fulfil personal desires for self or others—to developing a healthy, powerful, intimate and *effective* prayer life?

What I'm about to share with you may have previously been shared by others in different ways, but the truth of the matter is this—*If you don't **make** time to pray, then you won't have time to pray!*

I. **Follow these three simple steps to get started:**

   A. ***Set a T_____.*** Whether morning, afternoon or night. It's up to you! Pray about your special *time* to meet with the Father alone—*daily.* Be assured that He will never miss the appointment—so make sure you show up too! Write your special time for prayer below: (Mark 1:35)

   _____
   _____
   _____
   _____

   B. ***Find a P_____.*** Locate a quiet, secluded *place* in your home. Inform family of your prayer time and place so they do not disturb you unnecessarily. Write your special place for prayer below: (Matthew 6:6)

   _____
   _____
   _____
   _____

   C. ***P_____ daily.*** After you have committed to a set *time* and located your *place*, then get down to the work of *prayer!* Having a consistent *daily* devotional/prayer and Bible study time is a must for the believer. Write your plan for daily prayer below: (Matthew 26:36; Luke 6:12)

   _____
   _____
   _____

II. The bible tells us in 1Thessalonians 5:17 to pray *without ceasing*. What does this passage mean to you?

_____
_____
_____
_____

III. Below are some other *suggested* times to pray—*day or night*. Which of these places, or other places, do you find yourself praying the most?
- ✓ showering/bathing
- ✓ walking/exercising
- ✓ car—to/from work
- ✓ traveling/airplane
- ✓ mowing lawn/gardening
- ✓ cooking/housework
- ✓ carwash/laundry
- ✓ doctor/dentist office
- ✓ waiting in lines (grocery store; post office, bank, etc.)
- ✓ work (breaks, lunch, etc.)
- ✓ other scheduled/unscheduled times throughout the day
- ✓ morning—noon—evening—night

_____
_____
_____
_____

IV. When does prayer "posture" become important? (I Kings 18:42)

_____
_____
_____
_____

V. When you are ready to pray, how do you handle the following:
  A. "Wandering thoughts" or falling asleep? (2 Corinthians 10:5; Hebrews 4:11)

  B. Meeting God without an "agenda" or "to do list"? (Psalms 42:1-2)

  C. Shutting out distractions—*enjoy the silence.* (Ecclesiastes 3:7)

Time With God Prayer Agenda

"God speaks to those who listen; He listens to those who take time to Pray"

I. Period of Confession—*cleansing your temple.* (I John 1:9)

II. Prayer Focuses—*pray for the following:*
   A. Ask God to reveal *"His will"* to you on a daily basis through prayer and the study of His Word. Ask for strength to DO God's will daily.
   B. Pray not to *"grieve"* the Holy Spirit by indulging in known sin. Pray that the Holy Spirit will reveal any sin in your life—anything false, deceitful, hypocritical, doubt, unbelief, worry, anxiety, un-thankfulness, bitterness, unforgiveness, arrogance, pride, lukewarmness, spiritual dullness, worldliness, fleshliness, etc.—*then repent!*
   C. Pray not to hinder the Holy Spirit from manifesting himself fully within you because of sins of omission or commission. (John 14:17; Hebrew 10:29; Romans 1:4; Ephesians 1:17; 2 Timothy 1:7; I Peter 4:14)
   D. Pray the Holy Spirit will help you surrender to God what *He desires of you*—acceptable sacrifices. Pray for the ability to release your faith in *believing prayer*—totally trusting God to do what you cannot.

❧ *Spirit Inspired Thoughts* ❧

_____
_____
_____
_____
_____
_____

~A Personal Prayer of Consistency~

"If you don't Make Time to Pray, then you Won't Have Time to Pray"

Journal *your personal prayer of consistency* here. Ask the Holy Spirit to reveal any poor prayer habits you may have developed. Ask the Father to help you replace them with positive spiritual disciplines to develop a healthy, powerful, intimate and *effective* prayer life.

Psalms 37:4

_____
_____
_____
_____
_____
_____
_____
_____
_____
_____
_____
_____
_____
_____
_____
_____
_____
_____

In Jesus' name I pray, Amen.

A Twelve Step Personal Prayer Plan

"Then Jesus came with them to a place called Gethsemane, and said to the disciples, "Sit here while I go and pray over there." And He took with Him Peter and the two sons of Zebedee, and He began to be sorrowful and deeply distressed. Then He said to them, "My soul is exceedingly sorrowful, even to death. Stay here and watch with me." He went a little farther and fell on His face, and prayed, saying, "O My Father, if it is possible, let this cup pass from me; nevertheless, not as I will, but as you will." Then He came to the disciples and found them sleeping, and said to Peter, "What! Could you not watch with me one hour? Watch and pray, lest you enter into temptation. The spirit indeed is willing, but the flesh is weak." (Matthew 26:36-41)

INDEX

Step 1: **A**doration: Divine Praise & Magnification

Step 2: **C**onfession: Declared Admission

Step 3: **T**hanksgiving: Expressed Appreciation

Step 4: **S**upplication: Earnest Requests

Step 5: Waiting: Silent Surrender—Mind, Body, Soul

Step 6: Watching: Spiritual Awareness

Step 7: Intercession: Earnest Appeals

Step 8: Praying the Scripture: Pleading God's Promises

Step 9: Serenading God: Melodic Worship

Step 10: Meditation: Spiritual Deliberation & Evaluation

Step 11: Listening: Mental Absorption & Assimilation

Step 12: Total Praise: Unadulterated Worship

A Twelve Step Personal Prayer Plan
Moving Your Prayer Life to the Next Level

This *Twelve Step Personal Prayer Plan* is scripture based and designed to structure and increase your personal prayer time, develop consistency in your prayer life, and grow you in intimacy with the Father. In order to develop a healthy, powerful, intimate and effective prayer life, one must not only learn and put into daily practice the five lessons on prayer previously outlined, but equally important is the ability to use effectively all components of prayer.

Most Christians limit themselves to only certain aspects or elements of prayer—such as adoration, confession, thanksgiving and supplication (petition). These four basic elements are sometimes referred to as the four "A.C.T.S." of prayer—or the four steps of prayer. However, many believers do not experience a deeper and more intimate prayer life because they simply neglect to explore other realms of prayer. As I previously stated in lesson one of this book, *"Prayer is not just a way for us to get things from God—rather prayer is a way for us to get to God."*

Studying and putting into practice the previous five lessons and the following twelve steps of prayer will strengthen your personal relationship with the Father and usher you into a deeper realm of intimacy, catapulting your personal prayer life to the *next level!*

At the beginning of this book, you were challenged to open your heart and allow the Holy Spirit to expand your mind in order to experience prayer in ways that you never have before. This section is designed to help you do just that—equipping and empowering you to experience personal prayer beyond basic elements and the generic use of prayer.

As you study, meditate on and incorporate the twelve steps in this section into your daily prayer time, you will grow into a deeper, richer and more fulfilling relationship with the Father as you begin to pray spirit-led prayers with power, passion and purpose.

Step 1 ~ Adoration

Divine Adoration & Magnification
Psalms 63:3-5; Psalms 52:9

Many Christians have no idea how powerful praise is. When praise goes up, it causes a supernatural shift in the heavenly realms! The power of praise can be seen time and time again throughout the bible. Praise collapsed towering walls, *(Joshua 5:14-15; 6:2)* jolted jail cells, *(Acts 16:25-26)* and defeated armies. *(2 Chronicles 20:22)* Praise stirs up our faith and gives us the strength to stand against the enemy and weather the storms of life—not in our own power, but in the strength of the Lord. Most importantly, praise helps jump-start our worship experience!

As Christ followers, Jesus is our perfect example in all things—even in prayer. In Matthew 6:9-13, Jesus taught his disciples how they should pray. Many call this "The Lord's Prayer." However, I prefer to call it "The Model Prayer" because Jesus shared this way of paying with His disciples as an example of how to pray effectively—beginning by recognizing God's power and authority as you pray according to His will.

This method of praying is still our model to follow even today. Like Jesus' example, starting and ending your prayer time in adoration and praise is vitally important because it takes your focus off yourself (and your current situation) and puts your total focus where it belongs—on God. Starting your prayer time with adoration—praising God for *who He is*—and *s*eeking the Father first will open doors for blessings unimaginable! (Matthew 6:33)

For the study of ***Step 1: Adoration***, let's look more closely at the following:
- What is *adoration?*
- Why adoration and praise are both important in prayer.
- Seven Hebrew Principles of Praise.
- Compound or Covenant Names of Jehovah-God.
- Praising God's *Character*.
- Praising God's *Creation*.
- Praising God's *Word*.

I. **According to your understanding, *define* what the following words express as it relates to prayer:**
   A. *Adoration:* _____

   _____

Step 1 ~ Adoration

    B. *Magnification:* _____

    C. *Praise:* _____
_____

II. **Why is it important to make both *adoration* and *praise* a part of your daily prayer time?** *(Explain below)*

_____
_____
_____
_____

    A. Adoration ***ex*_____** to God from your heart how much you ***l*_____** Him. (Psalms 42:1)

    B. Praise ***u*_____** you into the very ***p*_____** of God! (Psalms 100:4)

    C. Praise jump-starts your ***w*_____** experience! (Psalms 63:3-5)

    D. Adoration and Praise helps you ***f*_____** on ***G*_____** alone. (Psalms 52:9)

III. **There are many different ways to express adoration and praise in prayer—some audibly and some silently.** *(Describe below how this can be done.)*

_____
_____
_____
_____
_____

    A. Why do you think it is important to learn various ways or methods of expressing praise and adoration?

_____
_____
_____
_____
_____
_____

A Twelve Step Personal Prayer Plan

Step 1 ~ Adoration

B. Try incorporating these *Seven Hebrew Principles* of praise into your prayer time. Which of these do you feel more comfortable expressing and why?
   1. *Yadah*—extending your hands. (Psalms 45:17)
   2. *Todah*—lifting up your hands. (Psalms 42:5).
   3. *Halal*—praising with instruments. (I Chronicles 23:5)
   4. *Shabach*—shouting Hallelujah! (Psalms 63:3)
   5. *Zamar*—singing unto the Lord. (Isaiah 12:5)
   6. *Barach*—praising God with a thankful heart. (Psalms 34:1)
   7. *Tehillah*—singing praises to the Lord. (Psalms 22:3)

   _____
   _____
   _____

IV. Learning to use God's *Covenant names* in prayer will help you focus on Him alone—expressing adoration and praise for *"who He is"* as opposed to petitioning what you desire. Why do you think this is important in growing your prayer life?

   _____
   _____
   _____
   _____

   A. Below are some compound covenant names of Jehovah-God to incorporate easily into your personal prayers of adoration—*praising Jehovah-God for His name!*
   1. *Jehovah-Jireh* (JI-RAH)—God your provider.
      (Genesis 22:14; Philippians 4:19)
   2. *Jehovah-Rapha* (RA-PHA)—God your healer.
      (Exodus 15:26; I Peter 2:24)
   3. *Jehovah-Nissi* (NIS-SEE)—God your banner of protection.
      (Exodus 17:15; 2 Timothy 1:10)
   4. *Jehovah-M'kaddesh* (MA-KAH-DESH)—God who sanctifies you.
      (Leviticus 20:8; I Corinthians 6:11)
   5. *Jehovah-Shalom* (SHA-LOM)—God your peace.
      (Judges 6:24; Isaiah 53:5)
   6. *Jehovah-Rohi* (RO-EE)—God your Shepherd.
      (Psalms 23:1)
   7. *Jehovah-Tsidkenu* (SID-KAY-NOO)—God your righteousness.
      (Jeremiah 23:6; 2 Corinthians 5:21)
   8. *Jehovah-Shammah* (SHAM-MAH)—God is present.
      (Ezekiel 48:35; Hebrew 13:5)

B. Which of the above *Covenant compound names* represent best who Jehovah-God is to you and why?

_____
_____
_____
_____
_____

V. Knowing Jehovah-God for *"who He is"* allows you to praise Him from a supreme perspective. (Psalms 40:11; Psalms 42:8; Revelation 1:8; 19:16)

    A. Learning to praise God's *c*_____ or nature expresses true adoration from the heart.

    B. Practice incorporating the following characteristics of God into your daily prayers of adoration—*praising Jehovah-God for His character!*

        1. Greatness, love, and mercy;
        2. Goodness and loving kindness;
        3. Holiness and righteousness;
        4. Truthfulness and faithfulness;
        5. Creativeness and understanding; and
        6. Omniscience, omnipotence and sovereignty!

_____
_____
_____

    C. Practice praising Jehovah-God for who He *has been and is* to you now!

        1. Wonderful Counselor, Mighty GOD!
        2. Everlasting Father, Prince of Peace!
        3. King of Kings, Lord of Lords!
        4. Alpha and Omega!
        5. Faithful and True!

_____
_____
_____
_____

Step 1 ~ Adoration

VI. **Learning to praise God's *creation* allows you to enter into a celestial period of praise—*Worshiping* not the creation, but the _C_____ of all! (Psalms 148)**

    A. Practice praising Jehovah-God *for His creation of...*
1. Sun, moon, stars and bodies of light;
2. Angels, heaven and height;
3. Waters, hail, snow and vapor;
4. Fire, winds, mountains, hills, trees and cedars;
5. Beasts, cattle, creeping and flying things and things of the sea;
6. Kings, princes, judges and rulers; and
7. Young men, old men, maidens, women and children!

_____
_____
_____
_____

    B. Begin incorporating some of the above elements of God's *creation* into your daily prayers of praise and adoration. What other forms of God's creation do you find yourself praising?

_____
_____
_____
_____
_____

VII. The Word of God and prayer are like two peas in a pod—they both go together!

    A. Having a powerful, effective prayer life is relative to knowing and applying God's _W_____ to your daily life. Learning to love, appreciate and praise *God's Word* in prayer is key to developing *i_____* with the Father.

    B. Praise Jehovah-God *for His Word.* (Proverbs 6:23; Proverbs 7:1-3; Romans 7:12)
1. His *law* is perfect—complete, total, absolute, whole, unbroken, and flawless.
2. His *testimony* is sure—certainty, definite, incontestable, and solid.
3. His *statues* are right—proper, correct, accurate, and sound.
4. His *commandments* are pure—unstained, unmixed, uncontaminated, and clean.
5. His *judgment* is true—real, good, accurate, faithful, upright, and authentic.
6. His *Word* is clean—spotless, stainless, pure, and lily-white!

_____
_____
_____
_____

C. Practice incorporating adoration for God's *Word* into your daily prayers. Journal a short prayer of adoration below:

_____
_____
_____
_____
_____
_____
_____
_____
_____

"Let everything that has breath praise ye The Lord!"
Psalms 150

Take 2 minutes to Praise Jehovah-God in prayer
Lord, teach me to praise and adore you more!

Step 1 ~ Adoration

Time With God Prayer Agenda

"The Word of God and prayer are like two peas in a pod—they both go together!"

I. Period of Confession—*a heart made pure and cleansed of sin.* (Psalm 66:17-20)

II. Period of Praise and Adoration!
   A. Praise God for *His love* and for His readiness to have a love relationship with you!
   B. Praise God for giving you a desire to pray and for strengthening your prayer life.
   C. Praise God for His *omnipotence, omniscience*, and *sovereignty!*
   D. Praise God for His generosity in making the *gift of prayer* available to you.

III. Praise God specifically for His name, character, creation and word!

❧ *Spirit Inspired Thoughts* ❧

_____
_____
_____
_____
_____
_____
_____
_____
_____
_____
_____
_____

~ A Personal Prayer of Adoration ~

"Praising God for who He is will open doors for blessings unimaginable!"

After reading and meditating on the scriptures below, journal your personal prayer of *praise* and *adoration* here:

Psalm 103:1-5; Psalm 150

_____
_____
_____
_____
_____
_____
_____
_____
_____
_____
_____
_____
_____
_____
_____
_____
_____
_____

In Jesus' name I pray, Amen.

Step 2 ~ Confession

Declared Admission
Psalms 139:23, 24

One of Satan's most effective tricks is to make the believer feel unworthy to ask for forgiveness. Because you may have fallen for that same, old trick or trap again, the devil's diabolical plan to make you feel too ashamed or embarrassed to confess and ask the Father's forgiveness—yet again—often times works.

However, *confession* must be a part of your continual walk with Christ. You must never let guilt or shame hinder you from saying, "Lord, I'm sorry—forgive me of my sin." Confession is agreeing with God about a wrong committed by action, thought, deed or neglect. Once you have admitted your quilt through confession, it frees you up to received God's forgiveness—and allows you to turn away from sin and return to a loving God (Matthew 6:12).

I. What does *declared admission* mean to you?
_____
_____
_____

II. Is *confession* and *repentance* the same? (Acts 2:38)
_____
_____
_____

III. Confession is conditional to *c*_____ your *t*_____ and preparing to receive God's abundant blessings. (Joshua 7:1-13)
   A. Remember, there can be no *h*_____ within, unless there is *c*_____ without! (1 Samuel 16:7; Proverbs 15:3; 2 Corinthians 3:17-18)
      1. You must *i*_____ deal fully with your personal *s*_____. (1 John 1:9)
      2. You must *a*_____ with God concerning your sins. (Psalms 66:18; Matthew 23:23-31)
      3. You must confess to God all *k*_____ and *u*_____ sins. Confess both sins of *o*_____ and commission. (Psalms 139:23-24)

B. Confession helps keep you *h*_____. Internalized *g*_____ adversely affects you mentally and physically. (Psalms 32:3)

C. Confession leads to *t*_____. You must admit your *g*_____! (Genesis 32:27)

IV. **Pray and ask God to reveal any *unconfessed* sins of commission or omission. Journal what is revealed here:**

_____
_____
_____
_____
_____
_____
_____
_____
_____
_____
_____
_____
_____

Confession is good for the mind, body and soul!

Take 2 minutes for Confession
Lord, teach me to confess my sins!

Time With God Prayer Agenda

"If your Christian life is a drag, then worldly weights may be holding you back!"

I. Praise Period! *Read aloud Psalm 103*

II. Period of Confession—a *heart made pure* and cleansed by confession and repentance of sin. (Psalm 66:17-20)

III. Prayer Emphasis—Pray to know God in a more *intimate* way:
   A. Pray to know God through His character, creation and Word!
   B. Pray to understand and appreciate the work of the *Holy Spirit* in prayer, and the way Jesus *intercedes* for you in prayers to the Father. (Hebrews 7:22-28)

❧ *Spirit Inspired Thoughts* ❧

_____
_____
_____
_____
_____
_____
_____
_____
_____
_____

~ A Personal Prayer to Admit Your Guilt ~

"There can be no healing within, unless there is confession without"

Journal your personal prayer of *confession* here: *Lord, cleanse and wash me through and through, so that I may live holy for you!*

Psalms 51:10-11

_____
_____
_____
_____
_____
_____
_____
_____
_____
_____
_____
_____
_____
_____
_____
_____
_____

In Jesus' name I pray, Amen.

Step 3 ~ Thanksgiving

Expressed Appreciation
1Thessalonians 5:16-18; Philippians 4:6

Jesus always gave "thanks" during prayer—whether raising Lazarus from the dead or blessing seven loaves of bread! As Christ followers—our perfect example—we should always endeavor to do the same. Thankfulness comes from having a heart of GRATITUDE!

The act of *thanksgiving* is expressing heart-felt gratitude to God for specific blessings He has bestowed upon you. When true thankfulness flows from your heart, you have a perpetual *attitude of gratitude*—not just circumstantial happiness. This means sincere thankfulness depends on what is in your heart—not just what is in your hand!

God's word says, *"Be anxious for nothing, but in everything by prayer and supplication, with thanksgiving, let your requests be made known to God."* (Philippians 4:6) This means your *thankfulness* is not tied to your existing state of reality or mentality, but rather your position with God—Abba Father!

I. **Thanksgiving is closely related to praise, but it is different in what way?**

   _____
   _____
   _____
   _____

   A. Praise focuses on *w*_____ God is—His character, nature and name.
   B. Thanksgiving focuses on *w*_____ God has done specifically for you.

II. **Expressions of thanksgiving can be mental, audible or silent. Why?**

   _____
   _____
   _____
   _____

III. **To truly express thanksgiving, you must learn to practice the following in prayer:**

   A. Start with a thankful *h*_____!
   B. Cultivate an attitude of *g*_____!
   C. Poses a *s*_____ of thankfulness!

A Twelve Step Personal Prayer Plan

    D. Remember—when you *T*_____, you *THANK!*

IV. Thanksgiving helps you focus on God's *f*_____. Learn to *c*_____ your blessings in prayer. Use the blank lines below each category to thank God for all He has done, is doing, and will yet do in your life!

    A. Confess *s*_____ blessings (e.g. salvation; growth; transformation, bible, etc.):
_____
_____

    B. Confess *m*_____ blessings (e.g. clothes; food; shelter, home, jobs, etc.):
_____
_____

    C. Confess *ph*_____ blessings (e.g. life, health, strength, sight, hearing, etc.):
_____
_____
_____

    D. Confess *fi*_____ blessings (e.g. incoming, outgoing and savings, etc.):
_____
_____
_____

    E. Confess *ex*_____ blessings: (e.g. church, family, friends, community, nation):
_____
_____
_____

    F. Confess *p*_____ blessings: (Thank God for what He has *already* done!):
_____
_____
_____

    G. Confess *f*_____ blessings: (Thank God for what you *expect* Him to do!)
_____
_____
_____

V. Thanksgiving in prayer is your special g_____ offering to God for all of His merciful kindness toward you! (Psalms 116:17)

Confessing your blessings!

2 minutes of Thanksgiving
Lord, teach me to give thanks always!

Morning Prayer of Thanksgiving

Thank You, Lord—for watching over me last night;
Thank You, Lord—for keeping me in your precious sight!
Thank You, Lord—for rocking me gently in the cradle of your arm;
Thank You, Lord—for keeping me safe from all hurt and harm.

Thank You, Lord—for I know that I am blessed!
Thank You, Lord—for sending me Your very best.
Thank You, Lord—for I know that my race is already won!
Thank You, Lord—because you sent to die for me your only begotten son.

So, I Thank You, Lord—for giving me this day!
Thank You, Lord—for Jesus—my light, my help, my hope, my strength for today!

Thank You Lord! Amen

By Mary A. Ford

Time With God Prayer Agenda

~ *Thank You Lord!* ~

"When I think about the Father's unconditional love for me—my heart leaps with uncontrollable THANKFULNESS!"

Journal *your personal prayer of thanksgiving* here. Time to confess your blessings! Confess past—present—and future blessings to the Lord.

Psalms 116:12, 17

_____
_____
_____
_____
_____
_____
_____
_____
_____
_____
_____
_____
_____
_____
_____
_____
_____

In Jesus' name I pray, Amen.

Step 4 ~ Supplication

Earnest Requests
Psalms 143:1; Matthew 7:7

We usually enjoy the presence of those we love—especially when they love us back! God loves you more than anyone else does, and it is a privilege to enter into His presence in prayer. God desires to meet your every need and is always ready to hear and answer when His children cry out to Him in prayer. (Jeremiah 33:3)

The act of personal supplication is simply pouring out your heart to God in sincere and earnest requests. Asking God to supply or provide your every need—Jehovah Jireh. It is petitioning God for your heart's desire!

"Ask, and it will be given to you; seek, and you will find; knock, and it will be opened to you. (Matthew 7:7)

I. **Asking God for *specific personal* things is not *un-_____*!**
   A. Jesus prayed prayers of petition and He is always our *e_____*. If supplication was necessary for Jesus, then how much more so for us. (Matthew 26:39)
   B. God promises to be Jehovah-Jireh—The Lord will *p_____*. (Genesis 22:14)

II. **When petitioning God, your *m_____* and *a_____* must be right! Read the prayer of Jabaz found in 1 Chronicles 4:9-10. Journal below why you believe God answered his *specific personal* request to be blessed:**

_____
_____
_____
_____
_____
_____
_____
_____

Step 4 ~ Supplication

III. Asking God to provide your needs expresses your *d*_____ on Him. Why would this be important in your relationship with God? (Matthew 6:11)

_____
_____
_____
_____
_____

IV. **There are four (4) keys to *effective* petition:**
   A. Be specific and *c*_____. In order to see specific answers, specific *p*_____ must be prayed! (James 5:13-16)
   B. Be *s*_____ in your requests. Personal *a*_____ matters—ask in the right spirit! (James 4:2-3)
   C. **K.I.S.**—Keep It Simple! Eloquence is not necessary for *e*_____ prayer. (Luke 18:13)
   D. Pray in *f*_____. Believe God can and will answer! (Philippians 4:19)

V. Which of the above do you *struggle* with most in your personal prayer time, when praying aloud or in a corporate setting? Why?

_____
_____
_____
_____
_____
_____
_____

You have not because you ask not!

2 minutes of Personal Petition
Lord, teach me to ask in faith!

A Twelve Step Personal Prayer Plan

Time With God Prayer Agenda

"You do not have because you do not ask God, your Father"

I. Praise Period! *Read aloud Psalm 100*

II. Period of Thanksgiving—*confess your blessings!*

III. Period of Petition: Pray that the Holy Spirit will help you to *release your faith* through believing prayer—trusting God to do that, which is impossible for man!
   A. Pray to become acquainted with God's many names and comfortable in using them when you pray prayers of petition:
      1. Elohim—the one true and only God; majestic ruler.
      2. El Roi—the Lord that Seeth.
      3. El Shaddai—the Almighty; all-Sufficient God.
      4. Jehovah Rapha—God our Healer.
      5. Jehovah Jireh—God our Provider.

❧ Spirit Inspired Thoughts ❧

_____
_____
_____
_____
_____

~ A Personal Prayer of Petition ~

"To receive specific answers, specific prayers must be prayed"

Journal your *personal prayer of petition* here. Openly and earnestly, ask the Father for what you desire—in faith!

Psalms 143:1

In Jesus' name I pray, Amen.

Step 5 ~ Waiting

Silent Surrender—Mind, Body & Soul
Isaiah 40:31; Psalms 46:10

When it comes to prayer—most believers associate "waiting" with being put on pause while in hopeful anticipation of God answering. This is a form of waiting in prayer. However, Step 5 focuses on *silent soul surrender*—not simply waiting on God to answer your prayer, but totally surrendering yourself to God as you wait on Him. This step helps you learn to *enjoy the silence*.

This practice of *waiting* in prayer is all about *total surrender to God*—mind, body and soul. Silently *surrendering* yourself to the Lord—everything that you are freely given to Him. During this time in prayer, the only words spoken should be "I love you Lord" or "I long for your presence, oh God!"

I. **What does *"soul surrender"* mean to you?**

    _____
    _____
    _____
    _____

II. **Why do you think *"waiting"* is a vital element of prayer? (Psalms 40:1-3)**

    _____
    _____
    _____

   A. Waiting helps fight the spirit of **s**_____. No **p**_____ ideas of how God should **a**_____ your prayers. (Matthew 26:39)
   B. Waiting helps you lay aside your personal wants in exchange for God's sovereign **w**_____. It helps you **s**_____ all—mind, body and soul to God! (Luke 22:39-42)
   C. Waiting gives you time to think only about the love of **G**_____ the Father, **J**_____ the Son, and the Holy Spirit. It helps you to get your **f**_____ right! (Psalms 39:7; 130:5)
      1. It helps to focus totally and completely on God's divine **l**_____ for you.
      2. It opens the door for you to **r**_____ God's divine love.

Step 5 ~ Waiting

    D. Waiting promotes a **s**_____ love affair with God! (Lamentations 3:25)

    E. Waiting prepares you for **_C_**_____. (Psalms 40:1)

III. Practice silently *waiting* in the presence of God—learn to **_e_**_____ the silence! Listen for God's still small **_v_**_____ and His whispers of love. Sense the promptings of the Holy Spirit. Journal your first experience of *waiting* in prayer below.

_____

_____

_____

_____

_____

_____

_____

_____

_____

_____

_____

_____

_____

_____

Lord, I surrender ALL!

****Take 3 minutes to Wait on God in prayer****
Lord, teach me to wait on you!

Time With God Prayer Agenda

"The child of God must be as ready to wait as to go, as prepared to be silent as to speak"

I. **Period of Confession**—*silently read Psalm 66:17-20.*

II. **Period of Waiting**—*silently wait before the Lord at least 10 minutes. (Psalms 40:1-3)*

❧ Spirit Inspired Thoughts ❧

~A Personal Prayer of Surrender~

"Lord, I love you enough to give you my all—mind, body and soul"

Journal your *personal prayer of soul surrender* here: Express to the Father your desire to completely surrender all and draw closer to Him—no preconceived agenda or strings attached!

Psalms 27:14; 33:20

_____
_____
_____
_____
_____
_____
_____
_____
_____
_____
_____
_____
_____
_____
_____
_____
_____
_____
_____

In Jesus' name I pray, Amen.

Step 6 ~ Watching

Spiritual Awareness
Matthew 26:41

Watching is a specific *element* of prayer that is very important but often times overlooked. It is reduced to simply *looking* for a specific *answer* to prayer. However, there is much more to watching when it comes to prayer. Believers must not only look for God's answer, but you must look for His hand moving in your circumstance—and be on the lookout for Satan!

"Be alert and of sober mind. Your enemy the devil prowls around like a roaring lion looking for someone to devour." (1 Peter 5:8)

❖ **Greek word for Watching = Gregoreo—to be awake or vigilant!**

❖ **Webster's definition for Watching = Keeping awake in order to guard: a close observation: or to be on the alert!**

I. **Watching *during prayer* means for all believers to…**
   A. Stay awake *s*_____ and awake *p*_____!
   B. Keep *g*_____.
   C. Stay *a*_____ during prayer!

II. **Why and what should believers be on the *lookout for* during prayer?**
   A. Spiritual *i*_____. (Matthew 26:41)
   B. Prompting of the *H*_____ *S*_____. (Romans 8:26)
   C. Divine *g*_____. (Colossians 4:2)
   D. Satan—the *e*_____! (1 Peter 5:8)

III. **Watchmen—Prayer Intercessors are often called *"Watchmen."* Why? (Isaiah 62:6)**

_____
_____
_____
_____
_____

Step 6 ~ Watching

A. Prayer Intercessors and all Christians *must*…
  1. Develop **h**_____ alertness.
  2. Be **s**_____ to the presence of God.
  3. Recognize the **p**_____ of the Holy Spirit.

B. Prayer Intercessors and all Christians must be **a**_____ of the various ways Satan tries to hinder the **e**_____ of your prayer life. (Ephesians 6:11-12)
  1. By having a dull and **d**_____ frame of mind while praying.
  2. Through **u**_____ of personal satanic attacks against you and your family, children and the church.
  3. Being ignorant of the wiles of the **d**_____ concerning his plans for you and the world.
  4. Praying prayers that lack **p**_____. Stay with the *goal* of your prayer.
  5. Making **s**_____ about prayer instead of claiming specific **p**_____ in prayer.
  6. Praying **r**_____ prayers or saying redundant words mixed in with your prayers.

IV. **Praying in the Spirit is a *"must do"* for Prayer Intercessors and all Christians alike. You must *i*_____ the Holy Spirit to *h*_____ you to pray. (Ephesians 6:18)**

A. **PRAYER FACT #1:** Human effort yields human results; but spiritual effort produces divine results (Nehemiah 2:1-8). In your own words write down below what this prayer fact means to you:

_____
_____
_____
_____

B. **PRAYER FACT #2:** Watching in prayer means opening your *spiritual eyes* to receive *divine* insight, guidance, direction and revelation from God concerning specific needs—both known and unknown. (2 Kings 6:17) Write down below some specific things revealed to you during prayer.

_____
_____
_____
_____

APPLICATION: Reflect back on today, yesterday or the past week. Watch for ways or methods used by Satan to hinder your spiritual walk. Write them on the lines below, and then prayerfully claim power to defeat Satan in each of these areas.

___
___
___
___
___
___
___
___
___
___
___
___
___
___
___

Use your Spiritual 20/20 in prayer!

3 minute prayer application for Watching
Lord, teach me to watch in prayer!

Time With God Prayer Agenda

"If you can't see God working in your life, then perhaps you're focusing on the wrong things"

I. Spend time *silently waiting* in the presence of the Lord. *Learn to enjoy the silence as you tap into your spiritual 20/20!* (10 minutes)

II. Ask the Holy Spirit to reveal further *spiritual facts* about your specific prayer requests—*then pray accordingly!*

❧ Spirit Inspired Thoughts ❧

_____
_____
_____
_____
_____
_____
_____
_____
_____
_____
_____
_____
_____
_____
_____
_____

~ A Personal Prayer for Holy Alertness ~

"We must stay alert to receive guidance and warn others of impending spiritual danger!"

Journal your *personal prayer for Holy Alertness* here. Ask the Holy Spirit to reveal hidden prayer needs for yourself, family, friend and your church—then pray for each need revealed as guided by the Holy Spirit.

Colossians 4:2

_____

In Jesus' name I pray, Amen.

Step 7 ~ Intercession

Earnest Appeals
1 Timothy 2:1-2

The act of intercession means praying to God on behalf of others—remembering others in prayer. Interceding on behalf of others in prayer to the Father is something Jesus himself modeled to his disciples in Matthew 6:9-13. In this model prayer, Jesus taught his disciples to pray for themselves and intercede for others. Therefore, Christians ought to follow his example: <u>Our</u> Father...give <u>us</u>...lead <u>us</u>...forgive <u>us</u>.

Intercession is the heart of prayer, as modeled by our Savior, Jesus Christ. Keeping this in mind, write your response to the following questions.

I. **Why is praying for *others* essential to your personal prayer life?**

_____
_____
_____
_____
_____

II. **How does prayer *intercession* get the believer involved in God's work?**

_____
_____
_____
_____

    A. World *E*_____—why should believers pray for salvation of the lost all over the world?

_____
_____
_____

    B. Engaging in spiritual *b*_____ on behalf of others—why is this important/necessary?

_____
_____

C. Reclaiming what the enemy has been/is **h**_____ back from the believer requires strategic **p**_____ intercession. How does this involve believers in God's work?

III. Prayer on behalf of the **un**_____ is clearly mandated, and modeled, by Jesus Christ in Matthew 6:9-10. The effectual **f**_____ prayers of the righteous avails much in the conversion of the lost. Therefore, evangelistic prayer should include praying for the following. Why?
   A. Believers/Christians:

   B. Evangelism events:

   C. Unbelievers/unsaved:

IV. The Apostle Paul models and encourages believers to pray for the **l**_____ in Romans 10:1-2 and I Timothy 2:1-4. Why do you think praying for the lost is so vitally important for the believer?

Step 7 ~ Intercession

A. Below is an acrostic that can be used to pray **b**_____ and **e**_____ for those whose *hearts* are far from God. Pray for their *HEARTS* to be changed.

Prayer for Their HEARTS

1. Pray for receptive and repentant **H**earts. (Luke 8:5-12)
2. Pray for spiritual **E**yes and **E**ars to be opened to the truth of Christ. (2 Corinthians 4:3-4; Matthew 13:15)
3. Pray they have God's **A**ttitude toward sin. (John 16:8)
4. Pray that they be **R**eleased to believe! (2 Corinthians 10:3-4; 2 Timothy 2:25-26)
5. Pray for a **T**ransformed lifestyle. (Romans 12:1-2)
6. Pray for God to **S**end them into the harvest field! (Matthew 9:35-38)

B. Prayer Intercessors must forget about their *own personal* **n**_____ and focus all their faith and prayer-attention on the needs of **o**_____. Why do you think this is true or not?

_____
_____
_____
_____
_____
_____
_____
_____
_____

Pray for their HEART to change!

3 minutes of prayer Intercession!
Lord, teach me to intercede for others!

A Twelve Step Personal Prayer Plan

Take the 4 x 4 Challenge!

Think about four (4) people you know who are unchurched or unsaved—then write their names on the lines below. Commit to interceding at least 4 times a week for these 4 people.

1   *Identify* 4 people who are unsaved or unchurched.

2   *Intercede* 4 times a week for these 4 people.

3   *Invest* time in building these 4 relationships.

4   *Invite* these 4 people to big events at your church.

Who are your 4 people?
1. _____
2. _____
3. _____
4. _____

Will *you* take this challenge? _____
                                              (Signature)   (Date)

Time With God Prayer Agenda

"Intercession is the HEART of prayer!"

PRAYER FOCUS: Intercede on behalf of friends, family, co-workers, supervisors, neighbors, spouse, children, etc. Pray a **BLESS-ing** on others in the following areas:

- ❖ *BODY (Physical)*—pray that the Father will bless them with physical health, well-being and abundance of life. (James 1:17)

- ❖ *LABOR (Work)*—pray for diligence in work, job security and financial blessings. (Proverbs 10:4)

- ❖ *EMOTIONAL (Inner Life)*—pray for their emotional health—release of stress, anxiety and depression from their lives. Pray they will have the "Fruit of the Spirit"—love, joy, peace, patience, kindness, goodness, faithfulness, gentleness, and self-control." (Galatians 5:22-23)

- ❖ *SOCIAL (Relationships)*—ask God to give them good relationships and friendships that will encourage them and not hinder them. (Ecclesiastes 4:10)

- ❖ *SPIRITUAL*—pray they will ask God for forgiveness of sins. Pray for their salvation and spiritual growth/walk with God. (Acts 26:18)

❧ *Spirit Inspired Thoughts* ❧

_____
_____
_____
_____
_____
_____
_____
_____

~ A Personal Prayer of Intercession ~

"Intercession is praying a BLESS-ing on those in need!"

Journal your *personal prayer of intercession* here. Pray fervently and confidently *name by name—need by need.* Then expect an answer when you pray!

Luke 8:5-12

In Jesus' name I pray, Amen.

Step 8 ~ Praying the Scriptures

Pleading God's Promises
Jeremiah 23:29

    Many Christians struggle with "how" to pray and for "what" to pray. The fact that God does not always answer prayers in the way or manner in which hoped, often times cause believers' faith to diminish. However, praying the scriptures—praying God's Word back to Him—assures that the believer is praying in the will of God and will receive the answer hoped for based upon God's Word.

    Praying the scriptures is simply pleading God's promises back to Him. Praying God's Word is the believers secret to receiving answered prayers. The degree to which you believe in God's Word and apply it to prayer, is the degree in which God will pour out His power in response to your prayers!

I. **What does *"faith appropriation"* mean to you? (Matthew 9:29; Luke 7:50; Hebrews 11:30)**

_____
_____
_____
_____
_____

II. **Read 2 Chronicles 7:14. Outline below the *"four (4) conditions"* and *"three (3) promises"* found in this scripture. Discuss how this scripture relates to answered prayer.**

_____
_____
_____
_____
_____
_____
_____

III. Why is it important to *f*_____ and pray as a believer? (Nehemiah 1:4; Acts 13:3; Mark 9:26-29)

_____
_____
_____
_____
_____

IV. To have an *e*_____ prayer life, it is important for the believer to incorporate *s*_____ into daily prayer time. Read the following scriptures, and then complete and discuss the statements below to help you understand *why*. (Luke 8:11-15; 1 Thessalonians 2:13)
   A. God's word must become a part of your daily *d*_____ time.
   B. Seek ways to bring God's Word directly into your daily *p*_____.
   C. Fasting long hours and prayer alone does not build faith—it takes God's *W*_____.
   D. The Word of God alone is the source of your *f*_____.
   E. The Word of God should be used to back your *p*_____.
   F. The Word of God is the *f*_____ for effective prayers.

V. We must learn to pray God's Word *b*_____ to Him! Read the scriptures below and the short prayers that follow. On the blank lines, complete each prayer by journaling your own petitions.
   A. *Matthew 6:8*—Father, You know everything I have need of even before I ask...

   _____
   _____
   _____
   _____

   B. *Psalms 34:10*—Lord, Your Word says those who seek You will not lack any good thing...

   _____
   _____
   _____
   _____

   C. *Psalms 24:1*—Lord, I praise You because everything in the earth belongs to You...

   _____
   _____
   _____

   D. *Psalms 50:10*—Father, every living thing was created by Your hand; including me...

E. *Genesis 18:14*—I know nothing is too hard for You, Lord…

F. *Ephesians 3:20*—I thank You, Father that you are able to do exceedingly, abundantly above all I can ask or think, according to the power that works inside me…

G. *Philippians 4:19*—Father, You promised to supply all of my needs according to Your riches in heaven…

H. *Romans 8:37*—Father, I thank You that no matter what trials I must face, I know I am more than a conqueror through Christ Jesus, who loves me!

I. *Romans 8:39*—Father, I thank You nothing can ever separate me from Your love!

Plead God's Promises back to Him!

Take 5 minutes praying the Scriptures
Lord, teach me to pray your promises!

Time With God Prayer Agenda

"Praying the scriptures is simply pleading God's Promises back to Him!"

Matthew 6:8 *"Father, You know the things that I have need of before I ask You!"*

Psalms 34:10 *"Lord, You said those who seek the Lord shall not lack any good thing."*

Psalms 24:1 *"The earth is Yours Lord, and all of its fullness!"*

Psalm 50:10 *"Father, every beast of the field is Yours, and all the cattle on a thousand Hills!"*

Genesis 18:14 *"There is nothing too hard for You, Lord!"*

Matthew 7:7 *"Father, You said to ask, and it will be given to me; seek, and I shall find; knock, and it will be opened unto me."*

Romans 8:32 *"Father, You did not spare Your own Son, but delivered Him up for us all, how shall then You not with Him also freely give us all things?"*

Psalms 37:5 *"Lord, You said to commit my way to You, put my trust also in You, and You shall bring it to pass."*

Luke 6:38 *"Father, You told me to give, and it will be given to me; good measure, pressed down, shaken together, and running over will be put into my bosom!"*

Ephesians 3:20 *"Lord, You alone are able to do exceedingly abundantly above all that we ask or think, according to the power that works in us!"*

Philippians 4:19 *"My God, You promised to supply all my needs according to Your riches in glory by Christ Jesus!"*

John 16:33 *"Father, I know that in this world I will have tribulation; but I can still be of good cheer, because You have overcome the world!"*

Romans 8:18 *"Father, I know the sufferings of this present time are not worthy to be compared with the glory which shall be revealed in us!"*

Romans 8:37 *"Yet in all these things, I know that I am more than a conqueror through Him who loved us!"*

Romans 8:39 *"Nothing can separate me from the love of God which is in Christ Jesus our Lord!"*

~A Personal Prayer Pleading God's Promises~

"The secret to answered prayer is how we apply God's Word during prayer"

Journal your *scripture-based prayer* here. Use scripture references to support your prayers as you journal—*pleading God's promises back to Him!*

Matthew 6:8

_____
_____
_____
_____
_____
_____
_____
_____
_____
_____
_____
_____
_____
_____
_____
_____
_____
_____
_____
_____
_____

In Jesus' name I pray, Amen.

Step 9 ~ Serenading God

Melodic Worship

"About midnight Paul and Silas were praying and singing hymns to God, and the other prisoners were listening to them. Suddenly there was such a violent earthquake that the foundations of the prison were shaken. At once all the prison doors flew open, and everyone's chains came loose" (Acts 16:25-26).

Singing has been used throughout the ages to express an array of emotions—happiness, sadness, joy, and sorrow. It has even been known to sooth the savage beast. Sometimes used as a vehicle singing releases sincere overwhelming gratitude, love, devotion and reverence. Praising and worshipping God in song combines adoration with a melody from the heart!

This act of melodic worship can be seen demonstrated in the bible—often used to win wars, defeat enemies, conquer cities and set captives free. God's military tactics often included *singing* as a strategy for the Israelites as they went into battle. As they begin to sing and worship, the Lord set ambushes against the armies invading Judah, and they were utterly defeated without the Israelites having to strike a single blow! (2 Chronicles 20:22)

Scripture tells us to *"Worship the Lord with gladness; come before him with joyful songs."* (Psalms 100:2) Singing songs to the Lord during prayer allows the believer to express that which cannot be put into words. It brings a special joy to you and God, but many often neglect it during prayer.

I. **What type of *songs* should you sing to God during prayer? (Ephesians 5:18-19)**

_____
_____
_____
_____

II. **Turn your favorite s_____ songs or *hymns* into prayers—a personal song offering to the Lord! Journal your prayer-song below.**

_____
_____
_____
_____

III. **Below are scripture references to help you reflect on what *type* of songs to sing unto the Lord. Try to fill in the blanks with the appropriate word description.**
   A. Sing songs of p_____ unto the Lord! (Psalms 135:3)
   B. Sing of God's *p*_____ and *m*_____. (Psalms 59:16)
   C. Sing songs of *t*_____! (Psalms 147:7)
   D. Sing songs about the *N*_____ of God. (Psalms 69:30)
   E. Sing God's *W*_____ back to Him. (Psalms 119:54)
   F. Sing a *n*_____ song! (Psalms 40:3)

IV. **Try singing songs inspired by the Holy *S*_____. Ask Him to create *new melodies* in your heart.**
   _____
   _____
   _____
   _____
   _____

V. **Singing is a *s*_____ *w*_____ weapon used in prayer! King Jehoshaphat appointed singers to go out before the Israelite army in battle and the enemy was totally defeated before they even arrived to the battlefield (2 Chronicles 20:20-22).**

   Question: How can you use singing during prayer to *win spiritual battles* in your life?
   _____
   _____
   _____
   _____
   _____

Give a special Song Offering to the Lord!

2 minutes to Sing unto the Lord
Lord, teach me to sing Your praises!

Time With God Prayer Agenda

"Praising God in song combines adoration with a melody from the Heart!"

~EXCERPTS FROM SONGS OF PRAISE AND WORSHIP~

Lord Prepare Me—to be a sanctuary. Pure and holy—tried and true! With thanksgiving, I'll be a living Sanctuary for you!

Oh Lord, My God—when I in awesome wonder consider all the worlds thy hands have made! I see the stars. I hear the rolling thunder. Throughout the universe, Thy powers displayed! Then sings my soul, My Savior God to Thee. How great thou art—how great thou art!

Oh, How I Love Jesus! Oh, how I love Jesus! Oh, how I love Jesus…because He first loved me!

Praise Him! Praise Him! Praise Him! Praise Him! Jesus—blessed Savior. He's worthy to be praised (repeat). From the rising of the sun, unto the going down of the same, He's worthy—Jesus is worthy! He's worthy to be praised! Glory! Glory! In all things, give Him glory! Jesus, blessed Savior, He's worthy to be praised!

I Love You Lord! And I lift my voice to worship you, oh my soul rejoice! Take joy my King in what you hear. Let it be a sweet, sweet, sound in your ear!

I Exalt Thee! I exalt Thee! I exalt Thee, oh Lord! (Repeat). Hallelujah, Hallelujah, Hallelujah, Oh Lord! (Repeat).

Lord, I lift Your Name on High! Lord, I love to sing your praises! I'm so glad you're in my life! I'm so glad you came to save us! You came from heaven to earth to show the way! From the earth to the cross, my debt to pay! From the cross to the grave, from the grave to the sky, Lord, I lift your name on high! (Repeat)

♪ *Spirit Inspired Prayer in Song* ♪

_____
_____
_____
_____

~A Personal Song of Prayer~

"Holy Spirit, create new melodies in my heart!"

Journal *your personal song of prayer* here. Perhaps you have a favorite *spiritual song* or *hymn*—try turning the words into prayers that express your heart's cry as you serenade the Lord in *melodic worship!* Allow the Holy Spirit to sing through you as you journal your prayer-song from the heart!

Psalms 100:1-2

In Jesus' name I pray, Amen.

Step 10 ~ Meditation

Spiritual Deliberation & Evaluation
Psalms 19:14

For the Christian, spiritual meditation is not the same as it is for followers of other religions. When believers meditate, the key is to concentrate and ponder on *spiritual things* as defined by biblical principles—intentional spiritual deliberation and evaluation. This type of meditation trains the believer to focus on God's Word and biblical truths in prayer.

The Hebrew word for meditate is *Hagah*—meaning to muse or to mutter upon. (Joshua 1:8) The Greek word for meditate is *Meletao*—meaning to be careful or to show care in a matter. (I Timothy 4:15) In both the Old and New Testaments, the word *meditate* has the same premise as a cow chewing on a cud. Ruminant returns of God's commandments, statues and laws over and over again in your mind and heart until they become a natural way of life!

"Let the words of my mouth and the meditation of my heart be acceptable in your sight, O Lord, my rock and my redeemer" (Psalms 19:14)

I. **What do you spend your time *thinking* about? Where does your *mind* wonder when you are not focusing on something *specific*? (2 Corinthians 10:5)**

_____
_____
_____
_____

II. **Explain the difference between *"spiritual meditation"* and *"yoga."* (Psalms 119:6)**

_____
_____
_____
_____
_____
_____

A Twelve Step Personal Prayer Plan

III. What does *"meditation"* and *"worry"* have in common? Which is more productive and beneficial to the believer? Why? (Philippians 4:8)

_____
_____
_____
_____
_____

IV. The following explicates the *eight (8) benefits* of spiritual meditation in the believers' life. Read each scripture, fill in the blank word, and meditate on the benefit. Then write down how each benefit helps to strengthen *your relationship* with God through prayer.

    A. Spiritual meditation helps to focus your *t*_____ on God Himself. (Psalms 62:5)

_____
_____
_____
_____
_____
_____
_____

    B. Spiritual meditation allows you to focus on God's *W*_____. (Psalms 1:1, 2)

_____
_____
_____
_____
_____
_____
_____

    C. Spiritual meditation helps to discover how to apply all the *t*_____ God reveals during prayer. (Psalms 25:4)

_____
_____
_____
_____
_____

Step 10 ~ Meditation

D. Spiritual meditation helps to apply spiritual *f*_____ and principles—as an individual and as part of the church body at large. (Psalms 119:105-106)

E. Spiritual meditation helps to focus on the *w*_____ of God—His creation! (Psalms 77:12)

F. Spiritual meditation allows you to focus on past *v*_____! (Psalms 143:5)

G. Spiritual meditation promotes personal inner *p*_____. (Isaiah 26:3)

H. Spiritual meditation allows you to see God's *p*_____ in proper perspective—through His eyes! (Jeremiah 29:11)

_____
_____
_____
_____
_____
_____
_____

Think Positive Thoughts—No Stinking Thinking!

2 minutes to Meditate
Lord, teach me to meditate on you!

Step 10 ~ Meditation

Time With God Prayer Agenda

"My meditation of HIM shall be Sweet!"

I. **Period of Meditation**—*ponder* on the scripture below word by word and phrase by phrase.

"Keep this Book of the Law always on your lips; meditate on it day and night, so that you may be careful to do everything written in it. Then you will be prosperous and successful."
(Joshua 1:8)

II. **Prayer Focus**—*Mediate on God:* His Character, His Word, His Love, His Faithfulness!
   A. *Pray* to receive new insight and revelation from God's Word each time you study.
   B. *Seek* God's wisdom to understand and apply His Word to your daily life.
   C. *Ask* the Holy Spirit to reveal specific times and ways of the Father's presence and power demonstrated in your life during difficult and joyous events. Write your thoughts below.

❧ *Spirit Inspired Thoughts* ❧

_____
_____
_____
_____
_____
_____
_____
_____
_____
_____

~A Prayer of Meditation~

"Waiting focuses on Loving God—Meditation focuses on Thinking about Him"

Journal *your prayer of meditation* here. Remember—the benefits of spiritual mediation far outweigh the burdens of worry!

Psalms 104:34

_____
_____
_____
_____
_____
_____
_____
_____
_____
_____
_____
_____
_____
_____
_____
_____
_____
_____

In Jesus' name I pray, Amen.

Step 11 ~ Listening

Mental Absorption & Assimilation
Ecclesiastes 5:2

There was a story told about a newly converted Commander of a Fighter Pilot Wing during the Vietnam War. Shortly after he became a Christian, he was scheduled to fly out on an early morning mission. That morning he got up a little later than usual which caused him to run behind schedule. Then before leaving the building, he realized he needed to stop by the men's room first. After washing and drying his hands. he threw the wet paper towel at the trash can, but missed. As he began to turn and walk out of the men's room, he heard a small voice whisper, *"pick up your trash."*

Well, because he was running late, he ignored the voice and proceeded to hurry out of the men's room down the hall to pick up the equipment needed for his mission—parachute, helmet, etc.—when he heard the voice again, but this time a little louder. *"It's your trash—go back and pick it up!"* Needless to say, by now the Commander was getting agitated. After all, he thought to himself, "I'm the Wing Commander—I've got airmen and janitors under me that can pick up trash!"

So, ignoring the voice a second time he hurried out to meet the van that would transport him to his bomb-loaded fighter jet. A third time the voice came, but with a more insistent tone, *"Go back and pick up that trash! It's your trash—now you pick it up!"* Finally, the Commander slammed down all of his gear to the ground, and furiously marched back into the building, down the hall to the men's restroom to pick up his wadded up paper towel and put it into the trash can.

He returned to his gear only to discover that the van left without him. Upon re-entering the building, he observed several officers and staff scurrying around and making phone calls. He asked what the state of emergency was. He was told the transport van had just crashed with another military vehicle—it exploded, and there were no survivors. In shock of the news, the Wing Commander bowed his head and whispered, "Thank you, Lord." Realizing if he had not obeyed that small, persistent voice inside, he too would have been a causality that day.

STORY MOTTO: *"God still speaks to those who listen—and He listens to those who take the time to pray."*

Listening during prayer is the act of mental absorption and assimilation. Effective personal prayer is a two-way conversation—not a prayer speech or monologue! If you will *listen* in prayer, God will reveal to you how not only to *pray effectively*, but how to *live effectively* for Him.

I. Listening in prayer is an act of both *d*_____ and *f*_____. Why?
_____
_____
_____

II. Believers humbly listen in prayer to receive spiritual *i*_____ from God. (2 Chronicles 33:10-13). Explain below why this is important in the life of the believer.
_____
_____
_____

III. How does the believer know if it is the *v*_____ *of God*, Satan or their own desires? (Deuteronomy 28:1-2)
   A. *Voice Test*—while listening in prayer your thoughts, impressions or instructions must pass the following assessments—*or* it could be the voice of *e*_____!
      1. Does it agree with *s*_____?
      2. Does it honor *G*_____?
      3. Does it *a*_____ or excuse?

IV. How does God *s*_____ to the believers in prayer? (Psalms 81:13; Job 33:31)
   A. Quiet *i*_____ upon your heart.
   B. A sense of God's *p*_____ gently leading you.
   C. Through His *W*_____.

V. How does the believer *p*_____ *to listen* during prayer time? (Jeremiah 29:12-13)
   A. Have your *B*_____ with you.
   B. Keep a *n*_____ handy for recording what you hear.
   C. Be *s*_____ in the questions you ask God.
   D. Allow God to *o*_____ your thoughts and steps!

Step 11 ~ Listening

Ask the Father to order your Steps!

2 minutes to Listen in prayer
Lord, teach me to hear your Voice!

Time With God Prayer Agenda

How to Hear God In Prayer

When listening in prayer, for good <u>reception</u> you must have the following four (4) attitudes:

1. **You must be *Quiet*.** You can't hear God if you're talking all the time! *"But the LORD is in His holy temple. Let all the earth keep silence before Him."* (Habakkuk 2:20)
2. **You must be *Calm*.** You can't rush God—no matter how urgent the matter. If you're frantic and babbling, you're not going to hear God speak to you. *"Be still and know that I am God."* (Psalms 46:10)
3. **You must be *Clean*.** Before you meet with God, you must take out your emotional, physical and spiritual garbage! Get rid of the garbage by confessing your sins to God and agreeing with Him concerning the error of your ways. Get rid of the stuff that stinks in your life! *"If we confess our sins, He is faithful and just to forgive us our sins and to cleanse us from all unrighteousness."* (I John 1:9)
4. **You must be *Humble*.** Be ready to do whatever God tells you from His Word—even if you don't understand "why." A prideful attitude will not work and it will block your reception! *"If My people who are called by My name will humble themselves, and pray and seek My face, and turn from their wicked ways, then I will hear from heaven, and will forgive their sin and heal their land."* (2 Chronicles 7:14)

Question: What is keeping you from hearing God's voice?

❧ Spirit Inspired Thoughts ❧

_____
_____
_____
_____
_____

~A Prayer Time of Listening~

"God speaks to those who listen—and He listens to those who take time to pray!"

Journal *your prayer concerning Listening* here. Pray for better reception while you listen for the Father's still, small voice. Remember—ask specific questions in order to get specific answers. Wait on the prompting and guidance of the Holy Spirit—then write down what you hear.

Proverbs 8:32

_____
_____
_____
_____
_____
_____
_____
_____
_____
_____
_____
_____
_____
_____
_____
_____
_____
_____
_____

In Jesus' name I pray, Amen.

Step 12 ~ Total Praise!

Unadulterated Worship
Psalms 52:9

Unadulterated worship is praise at the purest level from the heart—total praise! This type of praise is untainted by pride, untouched by arrogance and undiluted with grandstanding. This form of praise is pure, complete and uninhibited—freely exclaiming your innermost passions for the Father with fervency, honor, esteem and love. Praise stirs up our faith and enables the believer to stand against all odds!

Total praise is the act of divine adoration and magnification directed to God the Father. When entering this realm of praise, there is a clear and distinct recognition of God's holiness, sovereignty, omnipresence and omniscience!

I. Total praise is *r*_____ God's nature and praising Him because *of*...
   A. Who He _____.
   B. All He has _____.
   C. All He is _____ right now.
   D. All He will _____ do.

II. Meditate for about *30 seconds* on the following question and write the first five (5) responses that come to your mind.

"What has God done for you lately?"

A. _____
B. _____
C. _____
D. _____
E. _____

Time With God Prayer Agenda

PERSONAL APPLICATION

Most believers have no earthly idea how powerful our praise is in the heavenly realms. In total praise, we focus our spiritual eyes on God alone—seeing beyond ourselves and our current situation and problems.

Think about the previous question and the responses you wrote: *"What has God done for you lately?"* Now, begin to praise God uninhibitedly—for He is worthy of your UNADULTERATED PRAISE!

LET EVERYTHING THAT HAS BREATH PRAISE YE THE LORD!

**2 minutes to *Praise* the Lord! **
Lord, teach me to Praise you more and more!

~A Personal Prayer of Praise & Worship~

"Father-God...You are indeed Worship Worthy!"

Journal *your prayer of praise and worship* here. Remember—when praises go up…blessings come down!

Psalms 150

_____
_____
_____
_____
_____
_____
_____
_____
_____
_____
_____
_____
_____
_____
_____
_____
_____
_____
_____

In Jesus' name I pray, Amen.

POST-PRAYER QUIZ

INSTRUCTIONS:
Congratulations! You have successfully completed *"HOUR OF POWER: Moving Your Prayer Life to the Next Level!"* Now, it's time to see just how much your prayer life has grown since you began this course. Think about your personal prayer life. Where you were when you started this course, and where you are right now in it. Please be *totally honest* with your answers as you take this short post-prayer quiz.

1. I would rate myself as a _____ on a scale of 1 to 10 as a prayer intercessor or a person of prayer. (1 is lowest and 10 is highest)

2. My spouse (or best friend) would rate me as a _____ on a scale of 1 to 10 as a prayer intercessor or a person of prayer based on what they know *and* what I share with them about my prayer life. (1 is lowest and 10 is highest)

3. If I were to add up all the time I spent praying today (alone or in a group) my total time in prayer would be _____ (approximate hours/minutes).

4. My main reason *now* for praying is: (circle only <u>one</u> answer or fill in the "other" blank)
    a) To get something from God.
    b) To just enjoy time with God.
    c) To pray for someone else or someone I love.
    d) To check it off on my daily "To Do List."
    e) Other _____

5. I find myself praying more often *when*... (complete this sentence on lines below)
   _____
   _____
   _____
   _____

6. I probably *don't* pray more often because: (circle <u>ALL</u> that apply)
    a) I'm just too busy—not enough time in my schedule.
    b) I'm too tired to really focus when I try to pray.
    c) It's boring to me.
    d) I still don't know how to really pray.
    e) No one else in my house prays.
    f) I don't believe it makes a difference *or* that prayer works.
    g) _____
       (You fill in the blank above)

Five Lessons on Prayer
Answer Keys

What Is Prayer?

Lesson 1 ~ Answer Key

I. Let's start with the basics—first, define what you believe prayer *is* and what prayer is *not*:
   A. Prayer IS: *(fill in blanks with your own answer).*
   B. Prayer is NOT: *(fill in blanks with your own answer).*

II. **Pleading vs. Begging**
   A. *Communication, Conversation, Communion*
   B. *Talking and listening; Monologue!*
   C. *Righteous; plea*

III. **The Importance of Humility**
   A. *Heart*
   B. *God*
   C. *Pride*
   D. *Surrendered; Surrenders*

IV. **Seeking God's Face vs. His Hand**
   A. *Petitions; Communion*
   B. *Personal*
   C. *Hand; Face*

V. **The Power of Repentance**
   A. *Repentance*
   B. *Confession; repentance; away; to*
   C. *Repentance*

What Prayer DOES

Lesson 2 ~ Answer Key

I. **What does prayer do that causes Satan to tremble and be afraid?**
   A. *Connects; power source*
   B. *Access; power*
   C. *Equips; warfare*
      1. *Spiritual Warfare*
      2. *Battles; carnal*
      3. *Effectively; enemy*

II. **Do you have your War Clothes on?**
   A. *Word; prayer*
   B. *Faith*

III. **Cast all your Cares—I Surrender All!**
   A. *Burdens*
   B. *Access; warfare; surrender*
   C. *Prayer*

What's Hindering Your Prayers?

Lesson 3 ~ Answer Key

I. **Some *hindrances* to praying *effective* prayers:**
   A. *Sin*
   B. *Faith*
   C. *Motives*
   D. *Attitude*

II. **What's *hindering* your prayer life?** *(Fill in blanks with your own answer).*

What Effective Prayer Requires?

Lesson 4 ~ Answer Key

I. **What does effective prayer require?**
    A. *Work. Love.*
    B. *Seeking, knocking, searching*
    C. *Heart.*
    D. *Presence*

II. *Suggestion; Choices; Commandment!*

How Do We Get Started?

Lesson 5 ~ Answer Key

I. Follow these three simple steps to get started:
   A. *Time*
   B. *Place*
   C. *Pray*

II. The bible tells us to *"pray without ceasing"*…
   Fill in blanks with your own answer.

III. Which of these places, or other places, do you find yourself praying the most?
   Fill in blanks with your own answer.

IV. When does prayer *"posture"* become important?
   Fill in blanks with your own answer.

V. When you are ready to pray, how do you handle the following:
   A. *Fill in blanks with your own answer.*
   B. *Fill in blanks with your own answer.*
   C. *Fill in blanks with your own answer.*

Twelve Step Personal Prayer Plan Answer Keys

Step 1 ~ Adoration

Answer Key

I. **Define what the following words mean to you as it relates to prayer:**
   A. *Adoration*
   B. *Magnification*
   C. *Praise*

II. **Explain why is it important to make both *adoration* and *praise* a part of your daily prayer time?**
   A. *Expresses; love.*
   B. *Ushers; presence*
   C. *Worship*
   D. *Focus; God*

III. *Fill in the blanks with your own answers.*
   A. *Fill in the blanks with your own answers.*
   B. *Fill in the blanks with your own answers.*

IV. *Fill in the blanks with your own answers.*
   A. *Fill in the blanks with your own answers.*
   B. *Fill in the blanks with your own answers.*

V. *Fill in the blanks with your own answers.*
   A. *Creation*
   B. *Fill in the blanks with your own answers.*
   C. *Fill in the blanks with your own answers.*

VI. **Creator**
   A. *Fill in the blanks with your own answers.*
   B. *Fill in the blanks with your own answers.*

VII. *The Word of God and prayer are like two peas in a pod—they both go together!*
  A. *Word. Intimacy.*
  B. *Fill in the blanks with your own answers.*
  C. *Fill in the blanks with your own answers.*

Step 2 ~ Confession

Answer Key

I. *Fill in the blanks with your own answers.*

II. *Fill in the blanks with your own answers.*

III. Cleansing; Temple
    A. Healing; confession
        1. Immediately; sins
        2. Agree
        3. Known; unknown; omission
    B. Healthy; guilt
    C. Transformation; guilt

IV. *Fill in the blanks with your own answers.*

Step 3 ~ Thanksgiving

Answer Key

I. *Fill in the blanks with your own answers.*
   A. *Who*
   B. *What*

II. *Fill in the blanks with your own answers.*

III. **To truly express thanksgiving, you must learn to practice the following in prayer:**
   A. *Heart*
   B. *Gratitude*
   C. *Spirit*
   D. *THINK*

IV. *Faithfulness; confess*
   A. *Spiritual*
   B. *Material*
   C. *Physical*
   D. *Financial*
   E. *External*
   F. *Past*
   G. *Future*

V. *Gift*

Step 4 ~ Supplication

Answer Key

I. *Un-spiritual*
   A. *Example*
   B. *Provide*

II. *Motive; attitude*

III. *Dependence*

IV. **There are four (4) keys to *effective* petition:**
   A. *Concise; prayers*
   B. *Specific; attitude*
   C. *Effective*
   D. *Faith*

V. *(Fill in the blanks with your own answers).*

Step 5 ~ Waiting

Answer Key

I. *Fill in the blanks with your own answers.*

II. *Fill in the blanks with your own answers.*
   A. Selfishness; preconceived; answer
   B. Will; surrender
   C. God; Jesus; focus
      1. Love
      2. Receive
   D. Spiritual
   E. Confession

III. *Enjoy; voice*

Step 6 ~ Watching

Answer Key

I. Watching *during prayer* means for all believers to…
   A. *Spiritually; physically*
   B. *Guard*
   C. *Alert*

II. Why and what should believers be on the *lookout for* during prayer?
   A. *Insight*
   B. *Holy Spirit*
   C. *Guidance*
   D. *Enemy!*

III. *Fill in the blanks with your own answers.*
   A. Prayer Intercessors and all Christians *must*…
      1. *Holy*
      2. *Sensitive*
      3. *Presence*
   B. *Aware; effectiveness*
      1. *Drowsy*
      2. *Unawareness*
      3. *Devil*
      4. *Purpose*
      5. *Statements; promises*
      6. *Random*

IV. *Invite; help*
   A. *Fill in the blanks with your own answers.*
   B. *Fill in the blanks with your own answers.*

Step 7 ~ Intercession

Answer Key

I. *Fill in the blanks with your own answers.*

II. *(Fill in the blanks with your own answers).*
  A. *Evangelism*
  B. *Battle*
  C. *Holding; prayer*

III. **Unsaved; fervent**
  A. *(Fill in the blanks with your own answers).*
  B. *(Fill in the blanks with your own answers).*
  C. *(Fill in the blanks with your own answers).*

IV. **Lost**
  A. *Biblically; effectively*
   1. *Hearts*
   2. *Eyes; Ears*
   3. *Attitude*
   4. *Released*
   5. *Transformed*
   6. *Send*
  B. *Needs; others*

Step 8 ~ Praying the Scriptures

Answer Key

I. *Fill in the blanks with your own answers.*

II. *Fill in the blanks with your own answers.*

III. *Fast*

IV. *Effective; scripture*
   - A. *Devotional*
   - B. *Prayer*
   - C. *Word*
   - D. *Faith*
   - E. *Petitions*
   - F. *Foundation*

V. *Back*
   - A. to I. *Fill in the blanks with your own answers.*

Step 9 ~ Serenading God

Answer Key

I. *(Fill in the blanks with your own answers).*

II. *Spiritual*

III. **Try to fill in the blanks with the appropriate word description:**
   A. *Praises*
   B. *Power; mercy*
   C. *Triumph*
   D. *Name*
   E. *Word*
   F. *New*

IV. *Spirit*

V. *Spiritual Warfare*

Step 10 ~ Meditation

Answer Key

I. *Fill in the blanks with your own answers.*

II. *Fill in the blanks with your own answers.*

III. *Fill in the blanks with your own answers.*

IV. **Eight (8) benefits of spiritual meditation in the believers' life…**
   A. *Thinking*
   B. *Word*
   C. *Truths*
   D. *Facts*
   E. *Works*
   F. *Victories*
   G. *Peace*
   H. *Plans*

Step 11 ~ Listening

Answer Key

I. *Dependence; faith*

II. *Instruction*

III. *Voice*
    A. *Error*
        1. *Scripture*
        2. *God*
        3. *Accuse*

IV. *Speak*
    A. *Impressions*
    B. *Presence*
    C. *Word*

V. *Prepare*
    A. *Bible*
    B. *Notepad*
    C. *Specific*
    D. *Order*

Step 12 ~ Total Praise

Answer Key

I. *Recognizing*
   A. *Is*
   B. *Done*
   C. *Doing*
   D. *Yet*

II. *Fill in the blanks with your own answers.*
   A. – E. *Fill in the blanks with your own answers.*

About The Author

Mary A. Ford
*Author * Speaker * Teacher * Prayer Leader*

www.duty2delightministries.com

For Booking Information Contact Mary @ maford1958@gmail.com,
www.duty2delightministries.com or 817.784.6028

Mary is a native Texan and is a resident of Arlington, Texas. Mary is married to Reverend James A. Ford, Jr., and they both serve in ministry together at the Koinonia Christian Church of Arlington, Texas, where Mary is the Prayer Ministry Director.

Mary is not only a *Prayer Warrior* and *Prayer Leader*, she is also a *Teacher* of God's Word, having taught various prayer classes, bible studies and facilitated workshops on scripture based prayer for 20 years. Mary has received many awards and commendations in recognition of her faithfulness and Christian service. She has served as presenter, session speaker and prayer leader for various marriage conferences, women's conferences, prayer breakfasts and prayer revivals. Together with her husband, Mary has conducted workshops on *"Intimacy and Oneness"* and *"Praying Together to Stay Together"* as a husband-wife team.

In 2014, Mary authored her first book entitled, *"From Duty To Delight: Are You Enjoying Jesus Yet?"* which is a scripture based fifty-two week encouragement devotional divinely designed to provide a more in-depth "weekly" devotional experience for the believer. And as a result of this book, Mary was inspired to launch *"Duty2Delight Ministries"* in 2016 with the sole purpose of Christian discipleship—empowering, equipping and encouraging the believer to live a transformed life in Christ through the power of prayer.

Whether facilitating a workshop, teaching a class, speaking at a conference or leading a corporate prayer session, Mary expels such fervor, passion, enthusiasm, and conviction while moving audiences to embrace change through being hearers and doers. She captivates her audience while moving them to bring about positive, life-altering results in their lives.

Mary's workshops, sessions and classes on prayer have been described as INTERACTIVE, ENGAGING, MOTIVATIONAL, ENCOURAGING, and LIFE CHANGING. Participants leave equipped and encouraged to truly seek a more intimate relationship with God through prayer—thus moving their prayer life *"From Duty to Delight!"*

Most Popular Presentations

Hour of Power: Moving Your Prayer Life to the Next Level

An eight-week scripture based prayer curriculum designed to better equip Christians who have a desire to enhance their personal prayer life and pray more effectively. Participants will be challenged to…

- *Make prayer a priority in their lives,*
- *Develop consistency in their prayer lives,*
- *Learn to master various prayer elements, and*
- *Increase their personal prayer time with God*

Prayer That Works

An eight-week scripture based prayer curriculum that takes you on a journey through the powerful prayer life of the Old Testament Prophet Elijah. This course is designed to DEVELOP, STRENGTHEN and ENHANCE the believer's personal relationship with God through the power of prayer. Participants will be challenged to…

- *Make prayer a priority through increased personal time with God,*
- *Develop intimacy with God through consistency in prayer,*
- *Strengthen commitment to God through accountability and prayer partners, and*
- *Develop an effective prayer life—praying effectual, fervent Prayers That Work!*

Prayer Boot Camp 101

Learn to master the prayer basics through this 90 minute, power-packed prayer workshop. Participants will learn…

- *What prayer is,*
- *What prayer does,*
- *What hinders prayer,*
- *What effective prayer requires, and*
- *How to get started—developing an effective prayer plan*

Praying Together to Stay Together

In this 90-minute marriage workshop, participants will learn the power of prayer in marriage and—True ONENESS! Participants will learn…

- *How prayer deepens our relationship with God and one another,*
- *How prayer naturally brings couples into agreement with one another, and*
- *How to go before the Lord with our concerns in unity of heart, mind, and spirit!*

Prayer: A Prelude to Worship

This 90-minute workshop is designed to take your music ministry and praise team to the next level through the power of prayer and worship! Workshop goals and objectives:

- *Reveal the powerful connection that Christians have with God through Prayer,*
- *Explore the significance of prayer in worship, and*
- *See how prayer impacts personal and corporate praise and worship*

~Testimonials~
What They Say About Mary

"I had the opportunity to take a class taught by this author! Her book **From Duty to Delight** *has been instrumental in major life changes. Sister Ford breaks down reality and keeps our minds from the "what if's" of life. Thank you Mary Ford for the life changing experience!"*
~Denise Raddle, Classroom Participant

"Mary Ford has a long history in the Christian faith, prayer, and her allegiance to Jesus, the Christ. What a blessing 'From Duty to Delight' is to us! It's an easy to read, precise on point, and thought provoking work that's designed to help build one's faith. It invites the reader to think outside the box and view Jesus in a closer realm. I highly recommend **From Duty to Delight** *to readers of all genres."*
~Lois Snell, Author of **Renaissance of the Soul, In His Presence** and **Lineage**

"Mary Ford is a dynamic and anointed Intercessory Prayer Warrior! Have you read her book yet? You should." ~ Beth Bowland, Author of **Polaris**

www.ingramcontent.com/pod-product-compliance
Lightning Source LLC
LaVergne TN
LVHW061345060426
835512LV00012B/2570